OFFICIAL
Swansea City
Quiz Book

Volume 2

Gomer

Published in 2014 by
Gomer Press, Llandysul, Ceredigion, SA44 4JL

ISBN 978 1 84851 881 0

A CIP record for this title is available from the British Library.
© Copyright text: David Brayley 2014

David Brayley asserts his moral right under the
Copyright, Designs and Patents Act, 1988
to be identified as the author of this work.

Photography copyright acknowledgements

© Swansea City AFC
   pp. 22–23: 2, 3, 4, 6, 7, 8, 10; pp. 62–63: 1, 2, 4, 5, 8, 10
   pp. 102–03: 2, 3, 4, 6, 7, 9, 10; pp. 142–43: 1, 2, 3, 4, 5, 7, 8

© Gwyn Rees Collection
   pp. 22–23: 1, 5, 9; pp 62–63: 3, 6, 7, 9
   pp. 102–03: 1, 5, 8; pp. 142–43: 6, 9, 10

The publishers would like to thank Swansea City Football Club
for their co-operation in the production of this book.

Printed and bound in Wales at
Gomer Press, Llandysul, Ceredigion
www.gomer.co.uk

Dedicated to the people who have supported me on
my writing journey from the very beginning,
and continue to put up with my obsession and allow
me the time to continue with it – my family.
To my wife Debbie and daughters Georgia and Olivia,
thank you.

Introduction

I have been genuinely surprised and delighted with the response to *The Official Swansea City Quiz Book, Volume 1*. My plan when writing it was to produce a collection of quizzes and facts that would entertain and inform. The best comments I received were from people who said that, even in quizzes about periods in the club's history that they knew nothing about – often pre-World War Two – they learned so much about the players and events from the club's past that it gave them a different perspective. That is incredibly pleasing, because, as we know, history is changing and being made all around us all the time, but often, to understand and appreciate the future, we must learn about the past, which is what I have hoped these books will do.

Swansea City Football Club is enjoying its fourth consecutive season in the top flight of English football. This is a new record for the club, and a feat that was even beyond one of my boyhood heroes, John Toshack, who managed just two seasons at the top of the football tree in the early 1980s. However, when I started this second volume of quizzes, often digging through hundreds of facts about Toshack's Swans, the club's survival in the top flight under Michael Laudrup was in genuine doubt, and needed a catalyst to ensure it would not slip back in to the Championship. That was provided by the appointment of another club legend, Garry Monk, which paid an instant dividend with a crushing defeat over our relegation-doomed neighbours Cardiff City.

Fast forward six months, and Swansea have had a flying start to the new season, even competing for the top spot in the Barclays Premier League. That is an incredible achievement. When I think back to the research I did for this book about the dark days of the late 1960s and early 1970s, relegation to the Fourth Division, a fight for re-election to the league, crowds of fewer than 1,500 people, and then the problems of the early 2000s and that Hull City game, it speaks volumes for everyone involved with this club that they have been able to turn everything around so spectacularly to see the Swans competing at the highest level. I'm sure that every player, past and present, who is mentioned in the quizzes that follow, must feel enormous pride to have worn the white shirt. I feel a similar pride in being able to recognise their achievements in this book and thank them all for their contributions to the story of our club.

I would also like to thank Swansea City FC for their great support in creating this second volume of quizzes, in particular media manager Jonathan Wilsher for his continued help and encouragement. Thanks again to Gwyn Rees for the use of photographs from his private collection, and his support for both books. I am also extremely grateful to all at Gomer Press for believing in this project from the start and agreeing to publish a second volume of quizzes, and last but certainly not least, my editor (and Swans fan) Luned Whelan for her great professionalism and care in editing this book.

By the time you read this, our great club may no longer be sitting at the top of the best league in world football, and nobody knows what is yet to come. I just hope that this book will again help you learn about Swansea City's great past and provide an entertaining companion on the unknown, but no doubt exciting, nail-biting and nerve-jangling journey we'll all experience into the future.

I hope you enjoy the book.

David Brayley
Swansea
October 2014

Contents

Contents *(continued)*

Contents *(continued)*

Author's Notes: The club we now know as Swansea City was known as Swansea Town between 1912 and 1969. To avoid any confusion, all questions about players, managers, opponents, honours and anything else that has generated a question, sometimes relate to Swansea City, even if they are set in the period when the club was still called Swansea Town.

Unless specified, 'appearances' refers to league appearances and will include substitute appearances in any total quoted.

Transfer fees are notoriously difficult to obtain from clubs and, as a result, figures often differ between books, publications and websites. Therefore, any fees quoted in this book are to be taken as a 'reported' figure, where I have done my best to research the most accurate figure, but accept that this figure could be contradicted in various other publications.

All facts and questions in this book are accurate as at 15 September 2014.

Managers

Fact: *the Swans had seven permanent managers before appointing the first Welshman to manage the club. The manager given this honour was former Tottenham Hotspur and Wales captain, Ronnie Burgess.*

Questions

1. Who was the Scotsman who was player/manager of the club for 23 games between December 1985 and May 1986?

2. For which club did Paulo Sousa leave Swansea City in July 2010?

3. How many divisional championships did John Toshack win during his rise through the divisions between 1978 and 1981?

4. Who acted as the Swans' caretaker manager between Brian Flynn and Kenny Jackett in March and April 2004?

5. Which two clubs had Brendan Rodgers managed before joining the Swans?

6. Which former Swans manager led Doncaster Rovers to the League One title in 2013?

7. Of the following two managers, which one managed the Swans in the most competitive matches: John Toshack or Frank Burrows?

8. Former manager Kenny Jackett managed which club to promotion in the 2013/14 season?

9. Which two players were appointed joint managers of the club in March 2002?

10. Which club had Michael Laudrup been manager of in his last job before joining the Swans in June 2012?

Did you know?
The player who captained Leicester City to their first ever major honour, the 1964 League Cup, ended up managing Swansea City for 22 games. His name? Colin Appleton.

1912–1915: the early days

Fact: in the Swans' first season in the Southern League Division Two in 1912, the league was made up of 13 clubs. Ten of those were Welsh, with three coming from southern England.

Questions

1. The Swans were unbeaten in their first nine matches in the Southern League, but on 1 February 1913, they were defeated 3–1 at an away pitch that would in time come to be known as Roots Hall. Which club beat the Swans that day?

2. Walter Whittaker and Ernie Fisher made seven and 17 appearances respectively during the 1912/13 season, but in which position did they both play?

3. Billy Ball and Robert Grierson ended the first season in the Southern League as joint top scorers. Both played 19 games, but how many goals each did they score?

4. In which position did the Swans finish in the Southern League Division Two table in their first season of 1912/13, after winning 12 and losing five of their 24 games?

5. In terms of the Vetch Field, what was significant about the second home game of the 1913/14 season against Barry on 13 September?

6. Having won the Welsh Cup in 1913, the Swans made it to the semi-final in 1914, only to lose 2–1. But which near neighbours of the club knocked the Swans out?

7. The Swans became the first Welsh club to qualify for the FA Cup proper in 1914, defeating Merthyr 2–0 on 10 January. But which London club ended the Swans' run in a 2–1 away defeat on 31 January? The Swans were to beat them home and away in the 2012/13 Premier League season.

8. John William Bartlett became forever linked with the club's history on 8 May 1914. Why?

9. The Swans finished fourth in the 1914/15 season of the Southern League Division Two, but which English club, currently opponents of the Swans in the Premier League, finished that season as champions?

10. In terms of league appearances, which first did winger Amos Lloyd achieve for the club in the 1914/15 season?

Did you know?

There were nine other Welsh clubs in the Swans' first ever season in the Southern League Division Two in 1912, namely Cardiff City, Llanelli, Pontypridd, Mid-Rhondda, Aberdare, Newport County, Mardy, Treharris and Ton Pentre.

Answers

1. Southend United.
2. Goalkeeper.
3. Eight.
4. Third position.
5. The new Grandstand or Centre Stand at the ground was officially opened.
6. Llanelli.
7. Queens Park Rangers.
8. He was appointed the club's second manager.
9. Stoke City.
10. He became the first player ever to play in every league game of the season – the club's first 'ever present'.

5

Legends

Can you recognise the Swans' legends below from the briefest of descriptions? Each one is a different player, but left a genuine legacy at the club.

Questions

1. Born in 1951, I played 12 games for England and made 87 league appearances for the Swans, scoring 35 goals. The first club I played for was Birmingham City.

2. I played my entire career with the Swans from 1958 to 1975, making over 500 league appearances. I played three games for Wales and was one of the first footballers in professional football to wear contact lenses.

3. Swansea-born, with a Czech background, my Swans debut was as a 16-year-old in the Harry Griffiths testimonial against Everton in July 1978. I played 152 league games before joining Cardiff in 1985. I began as a full back but also played midfield.

4. A winger who became a full back, I played for the Swans between 1988 and 1993 and won six caps for Wales. I played for six other league clubs, including Cardiff City. I liked taking throw-ins.

5. I played for the club from 1952 to 1958. I played for Wales in the 1958 World Cup, and played over 300 games for Tottenham Hotspur. I won 59 caps for Wales, usually on the wing.

6. I began as a full back and ended as a central defender. After leaving the Swans I joined Crystal Palace, Blackburn and Fulham. My career was ended by a car crash in 2001 and I am now better known as a manager.

7. I was born in 1899 in Northumberland. I came to Swansea in 1920 and never left. I only scored seven goals for the club but played 586 league games – a record for an outfield player.

8. I had two spells with the Swans, and finally finished my career in 1971. I played for Wales and initially left the Swans for Sheffield United in 1961. I played over 600 career games and played lots of football with my brother.

9. I scored 77 goals in 143 league appearances for the Swans in my first spell at the club. I didn't play league football until I was 25. My favourite number is 10.

10. The Swans were my only league club and I played in every division for them. I was a hard-tackling right back and played for the club from 1971 to 1985.

Did you know?
In the 2007–08 season, five Swansea City players were selected in the PFA Team of the Year for League One. All five of the players – Ángel Rangel, Garry Monk, Andy Robinson, Ferrie Bodde and Jason Scotland – have made such significant impacts at the club that they are all quite rightly regarded as legends of Swansea City.

Answers

5. Cliff Jones.
4. Andrew Legg.
3. Chris Marustik.
2. Herbie Williams.
1. Bob Latchford.

10. Wyndham Evans.
9. Lee Trundle.
8. Len Allchurch.
7. Wilf Milne.
6. Chris Coleman.

Fact: the first time in the club's history that Swansea City played at Wembley was on 24 April 1994, in the League Trophy final sponsored by Autoglass.

Questions

1. The last time the Swans won the Welsh Cup in 1991, David Penney and Paul Raynor scored in a 2–0 win, but who did Swansea beat?

2. Which player was fouled for the first of Scott Sinclair's penalties in the 2011 Championship play-off final?

3. Which player partnered captain Ashley Williams in centre of defence in the League Cup Final win against Bradford City in 2013?

4. The Alan Hardaker Trophy is the name of the Man of the Match award in the League Cup final. Which player won it in 2013?

5. The Swans won the FAW Premier Cup on 11 May 2005, beating Wrexham 2–1, but what was significant about that match?

6. When the Swans won the League One Championship in 2007/08, they had three Spaniards in the playing squad. Can you name them?

7. Swansea City won the Autoglass Trophy in 1994, but can you name the victorious manager?

8. Which Swansea player was credited with an own goal for Reading in the 49th minute of the 2011 play-off final?

9. In the 2011 play-off final and the 2013 League Cup final, Stephen Dobbie and Michu respectively scored in exactly the same minute, which, coincidentally, was the exact same number that appeared on the shirt of the late Besian Idrizaj. In which minute did both players score?

10. By winning the 2013 League Cup final, the Swans qualified for the Europa League. Which was the first team they played in that competition in the third qualifying round on 1 August 2013?

Did you know?
The captain of Bradford City in the 2013 League Cup Final played eight league games for the Swans in the 1997/98 season. His name? Gary Jones.

Answers

1. Wrexham.
2. Nathan Dyer.
3. Ki Sung-Yueng.
4. Nathan Dyer.
5. It was the last match the club played at the Vetch Field.
6. Andrea Orlandi, Angel Rangel and Guillem Bauzá.
7. Frank Burrows.
8. Joe Allen.
9. 40th minute.
10. Malmo.

The 1920s

> **Fact:** in the 1924/25, season, when the Swans won promotion to League Division Two, their biggest victory of the season was a 7–0 home win against Brentford.

Questions

1. During the 1924/25 promotion season, which Swans player became the first ever to score five goals in one game in the 6–1 victory over Charlton?

2. Which inside forward with the initials H.D. made 319 league appearances, scoring 86 league goals for the Swans between 1922 and 1931?

3. In 1924/25, the season the Swans won the Division 3 (South) title, which Len scored 16 league goals in just 34 games?

4. Which of the following London-based teams did the Swans NOT play during that 1924/25 championship-winning season? Was it Reading, QPR, Clapton Orient, Charlton Athletic, Brentford or Millwall?

5. Newport County, Merthyr and which other Welsh club were in Swansea's division in the 1924/25 season?

6. Which feat did Jack Fowler and half back Bert Bellamy both achieve during the championship-winning season?

7. In which season of the 1920s did the Swans reach the semi-final of the FA Cup?

8. In that cup run, which heavyweight Division One side did the Swans beat 2–1 in the quarter-finals, in front of 25,000 fans at the Vetch?

9. In the semi-finals, which team from the north of England beat the Swans 3–0, so ending their cup run?

10. At which neutral London ground was that semi-final played?

Did you know?
When Joe Bradshaw, the manager who had won the championship and taken the club to the FA Cup semi-final, resigned for personal reasons in May 1926, the club didn't appoint a manager until the following March, believing the Board of Directors could do the job themselves.

11

The FA Cup

Fact: The first ever time the Swans met Cardiff City in the FA Cup was on 16 November 1991, in a first round match. The result was a 2–1 victory for the Swans at the Vetch.

Questions

1. Following the success of reaching the FA Cup semi-final in 1926, the Swans reached the sixth round in 1927 in another good cup run. But which Welsh club knocked them out at the first time of asking in the following 1927/28 season?

2. The Swans beat Blackburn Rovers and Stoke City before losing away to Sunderland in the 1954/55 FA Cup, but which Welsh international forward scored for the Swans in every round?

3. Who scored his ninth and last FA Cup goal for the club in the Swans' second-round victory over Brighton and Hove Albion at the Vetch, in a 2–1 victory on 6 January 1968?

4. In January 1970, the Swans were knocked out 2–1 by giants Leeds United at Elland Road. Which Swansea-born striker scored the Swans' goal, having scored four against Oxford City in the previous round?

5. The Swans enjoyed a cup run in 1979/80, but their third-round tie took three matches to settle, with the final one a 2–1 victory at a neutral Ninian Park. Which club were the opponents?

6. In the Swans' first season in the First Division in 1981/82, they drew Liverpool at home in the third round of the FA Cup. What was the score in that game?

7. Which then-Premier League side ended the Swans' brave cup run in the 1998/99 season, beating them 1–0 with a late goal at the Vetch in a fourth-round tie?

8. Division Two Queens Park Rangers were put to the sword by Division Three Swansea in the first round in 2001/02, but who were the four Swans' scorers in the 4–0 win?

9. Can you name the Blue Square Premier League club the Swans beat 2–1 in round three on 13 January 2009, after the brave underdogs had previously accounted for Swindon Town and Leeds United?

10. Which club did the Swans thump 4–0 at the Liberty in the third round of the FA Cup in the 2010/11 season, with goals from Monk, Pratley, Van der Gun and Sinclair?

Did you know?

The first time that the famous Double Decker stand was used in an FA Cup tie was in the 1933 game against First Division Sheffield United. With many fans locked out of the new 2,200 seater stand, the Swans couldn't take advantage of the extra support and lost narrowly by 3–2.

Good servants

The following are clues to players who were loyal servants to the Swans. To qualify, they all played 100 first team games or were at club for at least three seasons. Can you name them?

Clues

1. An excellent centre half, this local boy was signed quite late – aged 22 – from junior Swansea football and played 129 league games. Many believe that the knee injury he suffered in 1955//56 season cost the Swans promotion.

2. Possibly the most popular foreign player ever signed for the Swans. This Yugoslav international joined from Velez Mostar in 1980, and brought a flair seldom before seen to the Swans' defence in his 114 games until May 1983.

3. A charismatic goalkeeper during the dark days of the early 1970s, this Welsh international played 208 times between 1969 and 1974. Tragically, a car crash confined him to a wheelchair from 1975. Still fondly remembered.

4. A Busby Babe who, despite escaping serious injury in the Munich Air Disaster of 1958, sadly never got over its horrors. Having played for the Swans between 1961 and 1964, this talented left winger sadly passed away in November 2012.

5. A giant striker who joined the club from Bristol Rovers in January 1998, he scored 23 goals in 112 games in all football before joining Cheltenham Town.

6. A member of a Welsh football family, this player – equally at home in defence or attack – played 314 first team games between 1976 and 1984, scoring 72 goals.

7. A Swansea boy who played for Arsenal, Sunderland and Cardiff before coming home in 1958. He won 21 Welsh caps as a ball-playing centre half, although he often played up front for the Swans in his stints from 1957/58 to 1959/60.

8. A gifted winger, comfortable on either wing, joined the club as a Swansea Schoolboy, making 166 league appearances between 1959 and 1964, scoring 23 goals. Sold to Plymouth Argyle, he finished his career in Cardiff in 1971.

9. Accomplished left-sided centre back who played 174 league games for the Swans between 1997 and 2001. Remembered for his partnership with Jason Smith.

10. A real fans' favourite with a spiky temperament who graced both Swans' wings between May 1980 and January 1983, scoring 32 goals in all games. A Swansea boy, he came to the Vetch via Burnley, Derby County and QPR.

Answers

1. Tom Kiley.
2. Dzemal Hadziabdic'.
3. Tony Millington.
4. Kenny Morgans.
5. Julian Alsop.
6. Jeremy Charles.
7. Ray Daniel.
8. Barrie Jones.
9. Matthew Bound.
10. Leighton James.

Debuts

Fact: nineteen-year-old Willie Screen made his Swans debut on 7 October 1967, in the away draw at Aldershot. On 2 May 1969 against York City away, he was joined in the first team by his 17-year-old brother Tony, who went one better than his older brother by winning his first game 2–0.

Questions

1. Which member of the England 1966 World Cup-winning squad made his Swans debut on 16 September 1978, in an exciting 4–3 home win over Tranmere Rovers?

2. Who was the centre back who made his Swans debut on 10 April 1976 in a 2–0 home win over Southport? He would make his 257th and final league appearance for the club in 1987.

3. Which 18-year-old striker, signed from Bridgend Town and who would score 25 league goals for the club, made his home debut for the Swans in a 1–0 win over Bury on 2 November 1985?

4. Can you name the centre back signed for £10,000 from Tiverton Town who made his debut on 8 August 1998 in the home 2–0 win over Exeter City?

5. Leon Britton made his league debut for the Swans away against Exeter in a 1–0 defeat. But in which season did this debut occur?

6. Which striker, signed from Rochdale by Brian Flynn and who would score 16 league goals in 65 games for the Swans, made his debut in the away 1–1 draw at Southend United on 13 March 2004?

7. Which often inconsistent winger, signed for £60,000 from Queens Park Rangers, made his Swans debut on 19 February 2005, against Grimsby Town at the Vetch in a 0–0 draw?

8. Who was the heavyweight target man who marked his club debut against Tranmere Rovers on 6 August 2005 with the winning goal after 30 minutes?

9. In the first match of which season did Dorus De Vries, Ángel Rangel, Ferrie Bodde, Jason Scotland and Paul Anderson all make their league debuts for the club against Oldham away from home?

10. Which winger made his debut – initially on loan – on 10 January 2009, in a 2–0 away victory at Burnley? He was signed permanently at the end of that season and is still with the club.

Did you know?
On 15 June 1974, Giorgio Chinaglia made his World Cup debut for Italy against Haiti in the World Cup finals in Munich. Ten years earlier, in an away Football League Cup tie against Rotherham United, he had made his Swansea Town debut in a 2–2 draw.

Answers

1. Ian Callaghan.
2. Nigel Stevenson.
3. Sean McCarthy.
4. Jason Smith.
5. 2002/03.
6. Paul Connor.
7. Kevin McLeod.
8. Adebayo Akinfenwa.
9. The 2007/08 season.
10. Nathan Dyer.

The 1920s

Fact: in the Swans' first season in League Division Two in 1925/26, the title was won by a club called the 'Wednesday'. It was of course, Sheffield Wednesday, but the club were not renamed with their now more familiar label until 1929.

Questions

1. Joe Bradshaw resigned as manager on 19 August 1926, but who was eventually appointed as his replacement on 31 March 1927?

2. In May and June 1927, the Swans embarked on a overseas tour of Spain, and in so doing, they became the first British team to win a match in which Spanish city when they beat Catalonia Athletic 2–1?

3. On 17 September 1927, the Swans beat Wolverhampton Wanderers 6–0 at the Vetch Field, but which significant first, relating to the environment of the Vetch, took place that day?

4. In April 1928, which club was the first ever from Scotland to take part in a competitive match at the Vetch, when they played in a testimonial match?

5. In the 1926/27 season, in which famous reserves division did the Swans' reserves take part for the first time?

6. Can you name the heavyweight club from the north-west of England who beat the Swans 7–4 on 29 August 1927, only to be defeated 5–3 by the Swans at the Vetch just seven days later?

7. Which unwanted record was set by the club when South Shields visited the Vetch in a League Division Two match, in the rain, on 1 October 1927?

8. Goalkeeper Alex Ferguson and left-half Lachlan MacPherson shared which notable achievement in the 1927/28 season?

9. On 2 February 1929, Lachlan MacPherson scored once and had another goal disallowed in the 6–1 victory over West Bromwich Albion. But what had happened to him on the morning of the match?

10. Only one outfield player played in all 42 league games in the 1929/30 season. Can you name this wing half, who played from the Swans from 1924 until 1935, but who stayed with the club for many years after finishing playing?

Did you know?

On Christmas Day 1929, the Swans beat Notts County 3–2 at the Vetch. The very next day, the Swans travelled to Nottingham for the away game, and came away with a 0–0 draw. Additionally, both keepers in both games were related – Swansea's Alex Ferguson and his brother James.

Answers

1. James (Jimmy) H. Thomson.
2. Barcelona.
3. It was the first time the Double Decker stand was opened and used by the fans.
4. Heart of Midlothian.
5. The (London) Combination League.
6. Manchester City.
7. The lowest-ever Football League attendance at the Vetch to that point – 3,697.
8. Both appeared in every league game.
9. He got married.
10. Joe Sykes.

Jacks from abroad

Fact: the Swans have had several Dutch players in their ranks over the years, but the one who has made most league appearances for the club to date is Michel Vorm, who made 89 Premier League appearances, before joining Tottenham Hotspur.

Questions

1. When Dutchman Nico Schroder made his only Swans appearance against Stockport County on 27 August 1976, he became the third foreign player to represent the club in the league. But what position did he play?

2. London-born Reuben Agboola, who played 28 league games for the Swans between 1991 and 1993, won his nine full international caps for a country other than England. Which nation did he represent?

3. Which striker, who scored 10 league goals for the Swans in 44 appearances, also scored 19 goals in 66 full internationals for Jamaica between 1991 and 2001?

4. The Swans' first ever South American player was Giovanni Savarese, who scored two goals on his debut in October 2000 against Stoke City at the Vetch. But for which nation did he win 30 international caps, scoring 10 goals?

5. Mamady Sidibe was a popular player with the Swans during the 2001/02 season. For which African nation did he win 14 caps between 2002 and 2008?

6. Willy Gueret was a French goalkeeper who had played for Red Star of Paris and Le Mans before coming to the UK to play professionally. In which group of French-controlled islands in the Caribbean was he born in 1973?

7. Who was the Spanish Under-19s striker, signed from the Espanyol B team in 2007, who scored nine league goals in 49 appearances for the Swans?

8. Who was the manager who signed Dutch goalkeeper Dorus De Vries from Dunfermline Athletic?

9. Which Trinidad and Tobago striker, with eight goals in 41 international appearances, played for the Swans between 2007 and 2009?

10. The first Italian who played for the Swans did so in 1965, but who was the second, who appeared for the club 45 years later?

Did you know?
Besian Idrizaj, the immensely popular striker whose life was cut so tragically short, had won twelve Under-21 caps for Austria prior to joining Swansea City.

Answers

1. Goalkeeper.
2. Nigeria.
3. Walter Boyd.
4. Venezuela.
5. Mali.
6. Guadeloupe.
7. Guillem Bauzá.
8. Roberto Martínez.
9. Jason Scotland.
10. Fabio Borini.

SWANSEA CITY AFC

Picture Quiz One

Can you name all these players? Answers on p. 153

1.

2.

3.

4.

5.

6.

7.

8.

9.

10. _____ (Name both.)

The Europa League

Fact: when the Swans played in the first leg of the third qualifying round of the 2013/14 Europa League qualifying phase, it was their first competitive match in Europe since the humiliating 8–0 defeat against a star-studded Monaco team that contained Emmanuel Petit, Youri Djorkaeff and George Weah, in the European Cup Winners' Cup on 1 October 1991.

Questions

1. Which team did the Swans play in their first game of the campaign at the Liberty on 1 August?

2. Who were the three Swans goalscorers in that first match?

3. Which team did the Swans beat 5–1 in the first leg of the play-off round of the 2013/14 Europa League qualifying phase at the Liberty on 22 August?

4. Which Swans player scored two goals in the victory on 22 August?

5. Incredibly, the Swans enjoyed a 3–0 victory over Valencia in the first Group A match, but which three players provided the goals in that historic performance?

6. Who captained the Swans to that iconic 3–0 victory over Valencia?

7. Which other two teams, apart from the Swans and Valencia, made up Group A?

8. Which former European Champions League winner scored against the Swans during the group stages of the 2013/14 Europa League?

9. Three Swans players started all of the six games in the Swans' Group A fixtures, but only one featured in every minute of all six games. Can you name him?

10. Which player, with 285 appearances in the Barclays Premier League, came on as a second-half substitute for Napoli in the Round of 32 home-leg tie at the Liberty on 20 February?

Did you know?
The first person to get booked during the 2013/14 Europa League campaign was Jordi Amat after 47 minutes of the first leg of the third qualifying round. The first player sent off during the campaign was Leon Britton, who was dismissed in the 87th minute of the second leg of the play-off round for his second bookable offence.

Answers

1. Malmö.
2. Michu, Bony (2) and Pozuelo.
3. Petrolul Ploieşti.
4. Wayne Routledge.
5. Bony, Michu and De Guzman.
6. Angel Rangel.
7. St Gallen and Kuban Krasnodar.
8. Djibril Cissé.
9. Jordi Amat.
10. Pepe Reina.

The 1930s

Fact: in his 505th League game for the Swans – the final match of the 1933/34 season – Wilf Milne scored a penalty against Plymouth Argyle. If he had missed it, the Swans would have been relegated.

Questions

1. In which division did the Swans spend the entire 1930s?

2. The Swans had three managers during the 1930s. Can you name them?

3. Which Merseyside club attracted the highest league attendance at the Vetch – 19,604 – in the first season of the new decade on 3 January 1931?

4. At the end of the 1930/31 season, two players left the club after making over 700 appearances between them, scoring over 120 goals. Who were they?

5. Which player scored 16 goals in his first nine games for the club after joining for the start of the 1931/32 season? He actually failed to score in his first game!

6. What was the name of the Scottish goalkeeper who played for the Swans for most of the 1930s? He shared a name with a Scottish manager who would become famous over 50 years later.

7. Which unwanted record did the Swans team of 1933/34 achieve, something that had never happened to the club during a season before?

8. What was significant about Wilf Milne's goal in his 500th league game for the club in the home game against Lincoln in April 1934?

9. Swansea beat First Division Stoke City 4–1 in the third round of the FA Cup in January 1935. But which 19-year-old winger put Stoke ahead after just six minutes?

10. Which Swans legend retired in the 1935 season after making 313 League appearances?

Did you know?
In the fifth-round FA Cup tie against First Division Portsmouth on 17 February 1934, the Swans set a new attendance record with 27,920 fans turning up at the Vetch.

Answers

1. Division Two.
2. Jimmy Thomson, Neil Harris and Haydn Green.
3. Everton.
4. Billy Hole and Harry Deacon.
5. Cyril Pearce.
6. Alex Ferguson.
7. The team failed to win a single away game.
8. It was his first goal for the club.
9. Stanley Matthews.
10. Joe Sykes.

Shirt sponsors

Fact: *the Swans have had thirteen shirt sponsors since the first logo appeared on the shirts at the start of the 1984/85 season.*

Match the sponsor in the list below to the correct period in the club's history.

32 Red • Action • Diversified Products (DP) •
Gulf Oil • GWFX • M and P Bikes •
RE/MAX • Silver Shield • *South Wales Evening Post* •
Stretchout • swansea.com •
The Travel House (on two separate occasions)

1. 1984–1991

2. 1992–1993

3. 1993–1996

4. 1996–1998

5. 1998–1999

6. 1999–2000

7. 2000–2001

8. 2001–2004

9. 2004–2005

10. 2005–2007

11. 2007–2009

12. 2009–2013

13. 2013–2015

Did you know?

For the FA Cup fifth-round tie against Fulham in 2009, the club wore shirts sponsored by Paddy Power. After the game, all the match worn shirts were auctioned and proceeds went to NSPCC Wales.

Who am I?

Below are ten facts about a past or present Swansea City player. You get 10 points if you guess who it is from the first fact, and all the way down to one point if you don't guess correctly until the tenth fact. Answer given at the bottom – no peeking!

The facts

1. I am six feet (1.83m) tall.

2. I was born on 20 October 1983.

3. I was part of the winning squad of the UEFA Under-21s Championships in 2006.

4. I made my Premier League debut for the Swans in the club's first Premier League game at Manchester City.

5. During the 2010 World Cup, I returned home from the squad for two days due to the birth of my son.

6. An injury in my second season with the Swans restricted me to just 26 league appearances.

7. I did not play in the 2013 League Cup final, but was part of the match day squad.

8. I only missed one league game in the 2011/12 season, away at Stoke City.

9. The Swans signed me from a team called Utrecht.

10. I saved the first penalty the Swans ever conceded in the Premier League against Wigan Athletic at the Liberty Stadium.

Did you know?
Michel actually played a game in Holland's Eredivisie in the 2010/11 season, the week before he made his Swans debut against Manchester City. He kept a clean sheet in the game for Utrecht, away at VVV Venlo.

Michel Vorm

The 1940s

Fact: when the Football League suspended their leagues after three games of the 1939-40 season, the Swans joined a regional Division, along with Plymouth Argyle, Torquay United, Bristol Rovers, Bristol City, Newport County, Swindon Town and Cardiff City.

Questions

1. In the 1940/41 season, a reduced four-team south-west Regional League was set up. Which three other clubs, who had spent the previous season in Third Division South, joined the Swans in this mini-league?

2. Which future legendary England striker, who would score 23 goals in 25 England games after the war, guested for the Swans in a cup match on 26 April 1943?

3. What was the name of the Newport-based works team that featured in all of the Swans' wartime leagues from 1942, often attracting top league players as guests?

4. For the 1945/46 season, two 'Victory League' divisions called Football Leagues South and North were set up. The Swans finished 17th in the South Division, against the likes of Arsenal, Chelsea, Aston Villa and Tottenham Hotspur, but which 22-year-old future Wales striker scored an astonishing 38 goals for the club from his 41 games in the league?

5. When professional football proper resumed on a full professional league basis for the 1946/47 season, what division did the Swans reappear in?

6. The Swans and which other Welsh side were relegated in the 1946/47 season?

7. Wartime manager Haydn Green left the club in October 1947, but Billy who replaced him in the November?

8. The Swans became champions of which division by seven points in 1948/49?

9. In the 1948/49 Championship winning season, which former Cardiff City centre forward with the initials S.R. topped the Swans scoring charts with 26 goals?

10. What future club legend made his league debut for the club in the Boxing Day away defeat at West Ham United in December 1949?

Did you know?

In 1872, association football was played at St Helens when the Swansea Cricket and Football Club was formed. However, in 1874, a clause was inserted in the lease of the ground that professional football was to be banned, meaning only amateur rugby could be played. That ban remained in force until September 1940 when the Vetch was requisitioned as an anti aircraft site, and the club was allowed back to St Helens to play its wartime league football.

Answers

1. Cardiff City, Bristol City and Reading.
2. Stan Mortensen.
3. Lovells Athletic.
4. Trevor Ford.
5. League Division Two.
6. Newport County.
7. McCandless.
8. Division Three (South).
9. Stan Richards.
10. Ivor Allchurch.

Curt

> **Fact:** Alan Curtis managed the Swans in a caretaker capacity in 2004 for a period of 18 days, covering four games, winning one, drawing one and losing two.

Questions

1. Curt was born in the Rhondda Valley, but in which year?

2. When Curt first came to Swansea as a teenager, he was put in lodgings in Mount Pleasant with a former Swans legend and his family. Who was this legendary Swan?

3. How many times was Curt selected for the PFA Team of the Year whilst playing for the Swans? Was it three, four or five times?

4. In the 1977/78 season, Curt had the best goalscoring season of his whole career. He played 46 matches that year in all football. How many goals did he score?

5. Curt scored six international goals for Wales, but how many caps did he win? Was it 25, 35 or 45?

6. Curt left the Swans in June 1979 before re-joining in December 1980. Which club was involved in both those transfers with the Swans?

7. Apart from the Swans and the club referred to in the previous question, which other three league clubs did Curt play for?

8. In the Swans' first season in the top division in 1981/82, Curt played 40 out of the 42 league games. Only two players – a keeper and a midfielder – played more, 41 and 42 respectively. Can you name them?

9. How many separate spells did Curt enjoy as a player with the club?

10. The first game at the Liberty Stadium was Curt's testimonial match in July 2005. Who were the opponents that day?

Did you know?
Curt followed his mother's brother, who also represented Swansea and Wales before going on to play for one of England's biggest clubs, exactly as Curt did almost 30 years later. His name? Roy Paul.

Answers

1. 1954.
2. Harry Griffiths.
3. Three times.
4. 33.
5. 35.
6. Leeds United.
7. Southampton, Stoke City and Cardiff City.
8. Dai Davies and Robbie James.
9. Three.
10. Fulham.

The Robbie James Wall of Fame

Fact: *before the Sunderland game at the Liberty Stadium on 19 October 2013, the names of the second group of 20 players to be inducted into the Robbie James Hall of Fame were unveiled behind the south stand. There could be no better choice than Robbie to have such a tribute paid to him – a true Swansea City legend. Can you recognise some of the players from this second group of inductees from the details given about them below?*

Questions

1. A tough-tackling full back, signed from Manchester City in 1966. Made 178 league appearances before leaving in 1971. Returned to the club in the mid-1970s and worked in the commercial department, also becoming the stadium announcer at the Vetch.

2. Popular Irish keeper, signed from West Ham United in 1960. Made 140 appearances for the club. Best remembered for his heroics in the 1964 FA Cup quarter-final victory over Liverpool at Anfield.

3. Between 1965 and 1975, nobody played more games for the club than this Swansea boy, who played all his football for the Swans, making over 400 appearances. Went on loan to Manchester United in 1973, but never played for them.

4. Sixty-six goals in 233 league games marked this player, equally comfortable at centre half or centre forward, as a true Swans legend. When sold to Arsenal for £42,750 in 1959, it was one of the highest value transfers in British football history.

5. Didn't play for the Swans, but managed the club between 1991 and 1995, beating Wrexham in

the Welsh Cup final in his first season. He then won the Autoglass Trophy at Wembley in 1994. Resigned as manager in October 1995.

6. A pillar of John Toshack's back four during the climb through the divisions. Made Swans debut in April 1976, and made his 257th and final league appearance for the club 11 years later. Finished league career at Cardiff City.

7. Arrived at the club in 1924 from Sheffield Wednesday, and left when he resigned as assistant manager 44 years later in 1968. A great servant to the club, playing 312 league games. As a coach, also discovered Ivor Allchurch. Genuine club legend.

8. One of the few to have played for and managed the club. Made 205 league appearances from 1947–1954, then served as manager from 1967 to 1969.

9. Swansea boy, who played over 650 league games in a 19-year career, but even though only 98 of those were for the Swans, his high level of performance as an attacker in Toshack's Division One team helped secure his legendary status.

10. Product of Swans ground staff, this Merthyr-born converted midfielder forged his career as a full back, happy on either flank. From his 1991 debut, he made 165 league appearances for the club before departing to Huddersfield Town in 1995 for £275,000. Won 16 full caps for Wales. Now manager of Monmouth Town.

Answers

1. Vic Gomersall.
2. Noel Dwyer.
3. Geoff Thomas.
4. Mel Charles.
5. Frank Burrows.
6. Nigel Stevenson.
7. Joe Sykes.
8. Billy Lucas.
9. Leighton James.
10. Steve Jenkins.

The 1950s

Fact: *when Fulham visited the Vetch on 22 November 1952, the club fielded eight Swansea-born players, two from Ferndale and Newport respectively and a lone Englishman, born in Tamworth. His name? Gilbert Beech.*

Questions

1. In which division did the Swans spend the entire 1950s?

2. In the 1950/51 season, a 17-year-old goalkeeper made his Swans debut. He would go on to set a new league appearance record for a goalkeeper – 370 games. What was his name?

3. Which stalwart in the Swansea team flew to Colombia to sign for a local team in June 1950, only for the deal to fall through in an episode that became known as the 'Bogotà incident'? He was sold to Manchester City as a result.

4. During the 1952/3 season, the Swans fielded three sets of brothers. What were their surnames?

5. In February 1953 which Swansea-born centre-half broke his leg after making just 42 league appearances in his first four seasons at the Vetch?

6. Which former captain and record transfer signing at £11,000 was sold to Newport County in December 1953 after scoring 35 league goals in 205 games?

7. In the 1954/55 season, Ivor Allchurch topped the scoring charts with 18 league goals, but four other players scored ten or more. Can you name them?

8. In July 1955, the club's manager died in Swansea aged 61. What was his name?

9. Which talented and versatile forward was sold to Tottenham Hotspur on 2 May 1956 for £18,000?

10. During the 1956/57 season, which player scored at least one goal in nine successive league and cup matches?

Did you know?
When Cliff Jones was sold to Tottenham for £35,000 in February 1958, it was a British transfer record for a winger.

Answers

1. Division Two.
2. Johnny King.
3. Roy Paul.
4. Allchurch, Beech and Jones.
5. Tom Kiley.
6. Billy Lucas.
7. Harry Griffiths, Mel Charles, Terry Medwin and Cliff Jones.
8. Billy McCandless.
9. Terry Medwin.
10. Ivor Allchurch.

Fact: *Swansea boy Chris Coleman made his Swans first team debut aged 17. As a result, many people believe he was signed straight from school, but in fact, the club signed him from Manchester City in 1986 because he was homesick for Swansea after having joined the Manchester club as a YTS trainee.*

Questions

1. From which club did the Swans sign Alan Curtis in October 1989?

2. The scorer of Leeds United's only goal in their famous 5–1 defeat by Swansea in 1981 later joined the club from Burnley in 1985. Who was he?

3. Who was the future international defender signed as a free agent by Kenny Jackett from Telford United in May 2004?

4. In July 2007, the Swans paid £200,000 for Darryl Duffy, but which club did he sign from?

5. Which player was signed from Arsenal for £1 million in August 2012 on a three-year contract?

6. In the 2003/04 season, Swansea City signed 15 players, but only paid a fee for one of them, which was £35,000 to Rochdale for a striker who eventually played 75 games for the club, scoring 20 goals. Who was he?

7. Federico Fernández was signed by the club on 20 August 2014 for a reported transfer fee of £8m. From which club was he signed?

8. In which country was Jason Scotland playing his football prior to signing for Swansea City?

9. From which Bundesliga club did the Swans sign Itay Shechter on loan during the 2012/13 season?

10. Roberto Martínez joined Swansea City on a free transfer from Walsall. But which manager signed him for the club?

Did you know?

The Swans signed a former England captain and multi-European Cup and League Championship winner in 1983, whose previous club was Mansfield Town. His name? Emlyn Hughes.

Answers

5. Kyle Bartley.	10. Brian Flynn.
4. Hull City.	9. Kaiserslautern.
3. Sam Ricketts.	8. Scotland (with St Johnstone).
2. Derek Parlane.	7. Napoli.
1. Cardiff City.	6. Paul Connor.

The 1993/94 Football League Trophy (Autoglass)

Fact: the Swans won the 1993/94 Autoglass Trophy at Wembley, beating Huddersfield Town 3–1 on penalties after drawing the match 1–1. Most Swans fans will know that Roger Freestone was the keeper at Wembley that day, but can you name the other ten players who started the game for the club that day from the clues given below?

Questions

1. Right Back: signed as a trainee in 1990, would play 165 league games for the club before joining his Wembley opponents, Huddersfield, just 18 months later in a £275,000 deal.

2. Left Back: signed as a 20-year-old from hometown club Plymouth Argyle at the start of the cup-winning season, this cultured left back would play 119 times for the Swans before injuries forced him out of league football, joining Bath City in 1999.

3. Centre Back: playing just his third game for the club, this 21-year-old former West Ham United trainee only played in the final due to injury to Keith Walker. He would never hold down a regular place in the Swans' defence, and left for Peterborough United in 1995 after just 29 league appearances.

4. Centre Back: a firm fans' favourite after signing from Crystal Palace in 1989, he missed just 16 league games in his first five seasons. Spent his final season of league football in 1997/98 at Cardiff City.

5. Midfield: in the second season of his second spell with the club, this experienced Welsh international midfielder, who had first made his debut for the club as 17-year-old winger against Brighton and Hove

Albion in the First Division over ten years earlier, would spend two more seasons at the Vetch before drifting into non-league football.

6. Midfield: manager Frank Burrows' most loyal lieutenant, made 149 league appearances for the club, and lifted the trophy as captain at Wembley that day.

7. Midfield: making his 13th appearance for the club since signing from West Bromwich Albion seven weeks earlier for £15,000, this left-sided midfielder would spend a further four seasons at the club before moving to Leyton Orient.

8. Midfield: Merthyr-born attacking midfielder and sometime winger who scored 26 league goals for the club in 124 league appearances after joining as a trainee. Played one more season with the Swans before the club accepted an impressive £350,000 from Birmingham City.

9. Midfield: dimunitive winger, popular with the fans, whose best season for the Swans was 1994/95, when he scored seven goals in 43 league games. After a Swans career totalling 111 league appearances, he left for Walsall in September 1996 on a free transfer.

10. Striker: the scorer of the Swans' goal after eight minutes, this 6ft 4in target man left the Swans the season following the final, making just three league appearances in 1994/95 due to a back injury. Joined Scunthorpe United in August 1995 for £15,000.

The 1960s

Fact: in 1962, Glyn Davies from Derby County was signed, a former Swansea Schoolboy who had grown up playing football with John and Mel Charles at Cwmbwrla Park. He would later manage the club between 1965 and 1966. In his first season, his attacking approach saw an amazing 81 league goals scored, but unfortunately, 96 were conceded.

Questions

1. The Swans drew the penultimate game of the 1961/62 season, thereby avoiding relegation. The next and final game of the season was against that season's Division Two Champions, whom the Swans thrashed 4–2. Who was this team?

2. After several transfer requests, defender Mel Nurse finally left the club in October 1962 in a £25,000 deal, but which club did he join?

3. Which team did the Swans beat away from home in the quarter-final of the FA Cup in 1964? Despite having played there eight times, they had never won and had lost seven games.

4. The man of the match in that quarter-final was the Swans' goalkeeper who performed heroics throughout. What was his name?

5. At which neutral ground was the Swans' FA Cup semi-final held on 14 March 1964?

6. To which team did the Swans lose 2–1 in that semi-final, despite leading 1–0 at half time and famously being 45 minutes away from Wembley?

7. At the end of the 1963/64 season, which player was awarded a testimonial to celebrate his retirement, after 15 seasons and over 400 games for the club?

8. Another player who left the club at the same time was a goalkeeper who set an appearance record which would stand until 1999. What was his name?

9. Who was the future Italian international who made his Swans first team debut in the Football League Cup in October 1964, aged just 17?

10. Relegation to Division Three at the end of the 1964/65 season ended a run of how many consecutive seasons the club had spent in Division Two?

Did you know?
If the Swans had won their final game of the 1964/65 season away at Coventry City, they would have avoided relegation to Division Three and Portsmouth would have gone down. Unfortunately, they lost 3–0. It would be fourteen long seasons before the Swans would once again return to Division Two under John Toshack.

Answers

1. Liverpool.
2. Middlesbrough.
3. Liverpool.
4. Noel Dwyer.
5. Villa Park.
6. Preston North End.
7. Harry Griffiths.
8. John King.
9. Giorgio Chinaglia.
10. 16.

Moving out

> **Fact:** after Alan Curtis ended his third and final spell at the club in 1990, he moved out of league football and joined Barry Town.

Questions

1. To which club was defender Kyle Bartley loaned during the 2013/14 season?

2. In January 2011, striker Shefki Kuqi's contract with Swansea was terminated by mutual consent. But surprisingly, he soon joined which Premier League club?

3. Following the 2005/06 season, which player, who had made 122 league appearances for the club, scoring four goals, was released to join Chester FC?

4. Following relegation from the top division in 1983, and 393 league appearances, Robbie James left the Swans. But which club did he join?

5. Which Championship club did Kemy Agustien join in the summer of 2013 on a free transfer?

6. In terms of record transfer fees received for a player, which Swans player has been sold for the most money in a single deal?

7. Which popular Wales international midfielder, who now plays in the Scottish Premier League, was sold by the club to Norwich City for £250,000 in 2009?

8. During his spell at Swansea City, Stephen Dobbie was twice loaned to the same Championship club – which one?

9. Between 2003 and 2008, Andy Robinson became one of Swansea's most popular players. But which club did he move to in July 2008 after rejecting a new Swans contract?

10. Which striker, who played for the Swans in the Premier League, now plays for Toronto FC in the MLS, after a short spell in Turkey with Elazığspor?

Did you know?
In 1985, Swans striker Derek Parlane left the club after just 21 games. His destination was New Zealand, joining North Shore United.

Answers

1. Birmingham City.
2. Newcastle United.
3. Roberto Martinez.
4. Stoke City.
5. Brighton and Hove Albion.
6. Joe Allen.
7. Owain Tudur Jones.
8. Blackpool (was only loaned to Crystal Palace once).
9. Leeds United.
10. Luke Moore.

47

Which season?

Fact: in the season concerned, the total number of supporters visiting the Vetch Field in league games was 325,957, with an average of 15,521 per match. Can you name the season in which all the events listed below occurred?

1. Two former Swansea Schoolboys joined the ground staff, namely Mike Johnson and Barrie Jones. They would go on to make a combined total of over 300 league appearances for the club.

2. Harry Griffiths was the only ever present in the league with 42 appearances.

3. Ivor Allchurch was top scorer, with 14 league goals from 32 league games.

4. The first game of the season was a 0–0 draw away at Ninian Park in front of over 42,000 people. The Swansea team consisted of: King, Thomas, Jones (B), Charles, Peake, Brown, Allchurch (L), Griffiths, Palmer, Allchurch (I), Jones (C).

5. Regular players during the season included Mel Charles, Len Allchurch and Dai Thomas, and it was to be the final full season that Ronnie Burgess served as manager.

6. In the 4–4 draw with Fulham at the Vetch, keeper Johnny King was injured, so he spent the bulk of the match as a limping centre forward, with defender Bryn Jones taking over in goal.

7. Wales winger Cliff Jones was sold to Tottenham Hotspur in the second half of the season for £35,000 for, according to the club, 'persistent demands to play First Division football'.

8. Ivor Allchurch scored a hat-trick in a 7–0 demolition of Derby County at the Vetch.

9. After leaving the club for Arsenal as an amateur in 1946, Ray Daniel finally signed for the Swans from Cardiff City for £3,000 in March of this season.

10. In the final game of the season away to Bristol City, the Swans had to win to avoid relegation. They won 2–1, despite going behind in the first minute and having won only two away games all season until that point.

Did you know?

Throughout the 1950s, the Swans spent every season in Division Two. The only player that made at least one league appearance in every season from 1950/51 to 1959/60 was Len Allchurch, making a total of 252 league appearances and scoring 46 league goals.

Answers

The 1957/58 season.

Fact: in the 1965/66 season, the Swans' attacking commitment was proven, and they scored 81 league goals. 48 of those goals were provided by just three players – Jimmy McLaughlin, Keith Todd and Ivor Allchurch.

Questions

1. Following relegation to Division Three at the end of the 1964/65 season, the manager unsurprisingly resigned. Which former Swans player, aged just 33, was appointed on 1 June 1965?

2. The first signing by the new manager was to bring 36-year-old Ivor Allchurch back to the club in a £6,500 deal. Which club did he join from?

3. After one win in 14 games of the 1966/67 season, the manager was sacked. Which man, who had played 205 league games for the club between 1948 and 1953, was appointed permanent manager in his place?

4. After relegation to Division Four in 1967, which legendary Swan returned to the club as coach and chief scout after a spell as player/manager at Merthyr?

5. On 17 February 1968, 32,796 fans – a ground record that remained until its closure – packed the Vetch to watch the Swans play which club in the FA Cup?

6. Which defender re-signed for the Swans from Swindon Town on 8 June 1968, picking up where he left off after leaving the club six seasons earlier?

7. In April 1969, the Swans lost a two-legged Welsh Cup final 5–1 on aggregate. Which player scored three of Cardiff's five goals?

8. Which player, who had also left the Swans in the early 1960s, returned to the club in 1969, re-signing from Stockport and scoring seven league goals from the wing in his 45 league appearances in the 1969/70 season?

9. In the third round of the 1969/70 FA Cup, which Division One giants were almost shocked on their home ground when the Swans took the lead through David Gwyther, only for the referee to award a hotly disputed penalty and scandalously send off Mel Nurse, allowing the home team to scrape a 2–1 victory against the Division Four Swans?

10. The Swans ended the decade with a bang by gaining promotion from the Fourth Division, finishing in third place in the 1969/70 season. Which two players – a midfielder and a striker – topped the goalscoring charts, with 15 league goals each?

Did you know?
In the 1967/68 season, Ivor Allchurch, in his last season and aged 39, finished top scorer with 21 goals in league and cup, and played 45 games. A fitting end for the club's greatest player.

Answers

1. Glyn Davies.
2. Cardiff City.
3. Billy Lucas.
4. Harry Griffiths.
5. Arsenal.
6. Mel Nurse.
7. John Toshack.
8. Len Allchurch.
9. Leeds United.
10. Herbie Williams and David Gwyther.

One-season wonders

All the players below shone bright and briefly for the Swans, playing just one season for the club. Can you name them?

Questions

1. Started seven league games, making 18 league appearances in total as a striker for the Swans during the 2012/13 season, scoring just one goal. Joined Hapoel Tel Aviv for the 2013/14 season and has since moved to Nantes.

2. A full back bought from Worcester City for £12,000 who played every game in the 1992/93 season before being sold to Nottingham Forest for £375,000. Played 185 games for Forest, many in the Premier League.

3. A former Cardiff City midfielder, this hard-working player never really won over the Vetch faithful in his 14 appearances in the 1992/93 season after joining from Exeter in August 1992. He left at the end of the season to join Barry Town.

4. A popular, bustling striker who had made his name as a kid at Sunderland, he also played for Glasgow Rangers before eventually signing for the Swans in August 1992, making 33 league appearances with 12 goals before moving to Leyton Orient.

5. A former Liverpool player with over 400 league games, he played 36 games in the Swans' promotion season of 1978/79. Made a memorable impression on Osvaldo Ardiles in a League Cup tie at the Vetch.

6. Scored five league goals in 22 games between January 2010 and February 2011, this much-travelled Kosovan-born Finland international striker later played for Newcastle United.

7. A powerful 6ft 4in striker from Mali, he scored seven league goals in 31 games in 2001/02 after joining from CA Paris. He joined Gillingham for 2002/03.

8. Scoring two goals on his debut against Stoke in 2000/01 season, this Venezuelan international scored 12 goals in 31 league games before moving to Millwall for the 2001/02 season. He played for six MLS teams in his career.

9. Tough-tackling midfielder with over 600 league and cup appearances before being signed by Nick Cusack from Bury at the start of the 2002/03 season. Played 18 games in the league before falling out of favour under Brian Flynn.

10. Spent the 2011/12 season on loan at Swansea, making 26 appearances in the league in defence. Had previously been loaned to Yeovil Town and Bristol City.

Welsh Swans

All the players below made their full debuts for Wales whilst they were Swans players. Can you recognise them from the opponents against which they made their Wales debut and the date? Also given is their birthplace, position, the number of caps won during their career or to date, the date of their last game and finally, in brackets, the number of league appearances they made for the Swans.

1. Debut: Malta on 25 October 1978. Born Swansea. Midfielder. Forty-seven caps with seven goals. Last game: Yugoslavia on 23 March 1988. (482)

2. Debut: England on 17 May 1980. Born Cardiff. Attacking midfielder. Twelve caps with two goals. Last game: Brazil on 12 June 1983. (54)

3. Debut: England on 27 April 1982. Born Swansea. Centre back. Four caps, no goals. Last game against Norway on 22 September 1982. (257)

4. Debut: Holland on 14 September 1988. Born Slough. Centre back. One and only cap, no goals. (89)

5. Debut: West Germany on 15 November 1989. Born Swansea. Centre back. Sixty-five caps with three goals. Last game: Azerbaijan on 4 September 2004. (175)

6. Debut: Austria on 29 April 1992. Born Swansea. Full back or central defender. Thirty-two caps with four goals. Last game: Germany on 14 May 2002. (160)

7. Debut: Bulgaria on 29 March 1995. Born Whitley Bay. Midfielder. 2 caps, no goals. Last game against Georgia on 7 June 1995. (149)

8. Debut: Germany on 11 October 1995. Born Merthyr. Defender. Sixteen caps with no goals. Last game: Norway on 5 September 2001. (165)

9. Debut; Hungary on 9 February 2005. Born Aylesbury. Defender. Fifty-two caps with no goals. Currently still a member of the Wales squad. (89)

10. Debut: Estonia on 29 May 2009. Born Carmarthen. Midfielder. Seventeen caps with no goals. Currently still a member of the Wales squad. (127)

Did you know?

Roger Freestone, one of the club's greatest ever servants and holder of the club's appearance record for a goalkeeper, made his debut for Wales as a 32-year-old on 23 May 2000. Proudly taking the field as a Swans player, Freestone wasn't to know that it was to be his only cap for his country. But what a country to win your only cap against – Brazil!

Answers

1. Robbie James.
2. David Giles.
3. Nigel Stevenson.
4. Alan Knill.
5. Andy Melville.
6. Chris Coleman.
7. John Cornforth.
8. Steve Jenkins.
9. Sam Ricketts.
10. Joe Allen.

Fact: *in August 1973, winger Brian Evans was sold to Hereford for £7,000, and a shrewd profit on the £750 he was bought for in 1963, some 355 league appearances earlier.*

Questions

1. Prior to the 1973/74 season, David Gwyther, the club's top scorer in the previous four seasons, was sold for a bargain £12,000, to which club?

2. From the money received from Gwyther's sale, manager Harry Gregg paid Bristol City a combined fee of £10,000 for a centre back and a left-sided player who would become firm favourites at the club. Can you name both?

3. Which young full-back was appointed to the role of club captain for the 1973/74 season? He would remain with the club for many years.

4. Which record was set in the match at the Vetch versus Northampton Town on 18 September 1973?

5. Jimmy Rimmer joined the Swans on loan for 17 games in 1973 from which club?

6. When the Swans drew 3–3 with Doncaster Rovers on 7 September 1974, Geoff Thomas did something no Swans player had done since the game against Grimsby Town on 7 October 1972. What was it?

7. In January 1975, manager Harry Gregg resigned to take over at which club?

8. Which former Swans player was appointed to replace Gregg?

9. Which legal formality did the club have to make at the end of the 1974/75 season?

10. In 1974/75, a season where just 46 league goals were scored, which two players were joint top marksman with eight each? One had played over 300 league games for the club, the other fewer than 70.

Did you know?
Prior to the 1974/75 season, just 612 season tickets were sold by the club, the lowest since the end of World War Two.

Answers

1. Halifax Town.
2. Dave Bruton and Danny Bartley.
3. Wyndham Evans.
4. It was the lowest recorded attendance for a first team match – 1,301.
5. Manchester United.
6. Score a hat-trick (Geoff Thomas was also the last).
7. Crewe Alexandra.
8. Harry Griffiths.
9. They had to apply for re-election to the Football League.
10. Geoff Thomas and Robbie James.

SWANSEA CITY AFC

The FA Cup

Fact: in the Swans' first ever season in the FA Cup in 1913/14, they experienced one of their best ever cup runs, winning seven consecutive ties. However, as six of those were qualifying rounds, they only won one round proper, against Merthyr Town. In the next round they were drawn against Queens Park Rangers, losing 2–1 to their Southern League rivals.

Questions

1. The Swans played their first ever match in the FA Cup in a pre-qualifying round tie on 27 September 1913, which saw the Swans run out comfortable 4–0 winners. But which near neighbours, who currently play in the Welsh Premier League, did they beat?

2. Who were the Northamptonshire based non-league team who knocked the Swans out of the FA Cup in December 1974 in a first-round replay after holding the Swans 1–1 at the Vetch?

3. In the 1983/84 FA Cup, the Swans were knocked out 2–0 in the third round by the previous season's runners up. Who were they?

4. On 21 November 1984, the Swans suffered yet another humiliating FA Cup upset at the hands of non-league opposition in a first-round replay. Which English south coast team beat the Swans 3–1 that day, with the Swans' only goal being scored by Chris Marustik?

5. Who was the Beazer Homes League side from the Midlands who performed another giant-killing act on the Swans in an away first-round replay on 23 November 1993?

6. In the 1998/99 FA Cup, which then-Second Division side, but now a longtime Premier League club, did the Swans dispatch 1–0 in a second-round tie at the Vetch, with the winning goal coming from Ritchie Appleby?

7. Who scored the winning goal against Premier League West Ham United at the Vetch in a third round replay on 13 January 1999?

8. The Swans enjoyed a long cup run in 2003/04, beating Rushden & Diamonds, Stevenage Borough, Macclesfield Town and Preston North End, before a brave 2–1 away defeat in the fifth round to a Second Division club, but which one?

9. The last ever FA Cup tie played at the Vetch on 17 January 2005 saw the Swans bow out to a Championship side that the League Two Swans had bravely held to a 1–1 away draw a week earlier. Who was this side, who knocked the Swans out with a last-minute goal from Nicky Forster?

10. The 2006/07 cup run saw the Swans knock out Premier League Sheffield United at Bramall Lane in the third round. Which two men supplied the three winning Swans goals in just 14 minutes in the second half?

Did you know? In the third round of the FA Cup in January 1935, the Swans outclassed Stoke City at the Vetch 4–1, but the scorer of the only Stoke goal caught the eye – a 16-year-old called Stanley Matthews.

Answers

1. Port Talbot.
2. Kettering.
3. Brighton and Hove Albion.
4. Bognor Regis.
5. Nuneaton Borough.
6. Stoke City.
7. Martin Thomas.
8. Tranmere Rovers.
9. Reading.
10. Tom Butler (2) and Leon Britton (pen).

Jacks from abroad

Fact: *Andrea Orlandi, who made 72 league appearances for the club, actually made one appearance for Barcelona (against Athletic Bilbao) in May 2006, on the day the Spanish giants were crowned La Liga champions.*

Questions

1. The fifth overseas player to represent the club was Ante Rajković, one of the club's finest ever centre backs. But what nationality was he?

2. Who was the first Scandinavian to play a first team game for the Swans?

3. Nicolas Fabiano was a French Under-21 international who played 16 league games for the club in League Division Two in the 2000/01 season. But from which French Ligue 1 side was he on loan to the Swans?

4. Who was the first Spaniard to play for Swansea City?

5. Rory Fallon was the first player from which country to play first team football for the Swans?

6. For which club had Ferrie Bodde made 159 appearances prior to signing for the Swans in 2007?

7. What nationality was Fede Bessone, who enjoyed two spells with club, making 37 league appearances in total, including one in the Premier League?

8. Prior to signing for the Swans in 2010, for which other British side had Dutch Under-21 international Kemy Agustien previously played on loan in the 2008/09 season?

9. Wilfried Bony is the club's first player from the Ivory Coast. Which European club did he join in 2007, when he first left Africa?

10. Striker Tamás Priskin had a short loan spell with the club in 2011, making four substitute appearances and scoring a single goal. For which nation has he won 42 caps since 2005?

Did you know?
Despite being born in London, popular Swans centre back Kevin Austin made his international debut for Trinidad and Tobago in 2000, against Panama.

Answers

1. Yugoslavian.
2. Jan Molby.
3. Paris St. Germain.
4. Roberto Martinez.
5. New Zealand.
6. ADO Den Haag.
7. Argentinian.
8. Birmingham City.
9. Sparta Prague.
10. Hungary.

61

SWANSEA CITY AFC

Picture Quiz Two

Can you name all these players? Answers on p. 153

1.

2.

3.

4.

5.

6.

7.

8.

9.

10.

Nicknames

In February 2013, in the run-up to the Capital One Cup final, then club skipper Garry Monk gave a newspaper interview where he revealed the nicknames of players in the squad.

Can you recognise them below from Monk's descriptions?

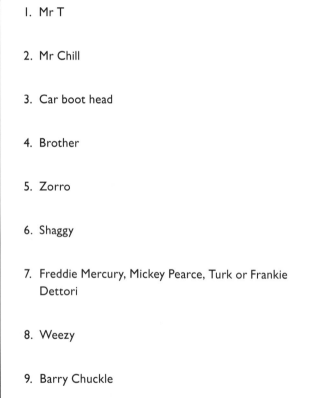

1. Mr T

2. Mr Chill

3. Car boot head

4. Brother

5. Zorro

6. Shaggy

7. Freddie Mercury, Mickey Pearce, Turk or Frankie Dettori

8. Weezy

9. Barry Chuckle

10. Chris Rock

Did you know?

One of the most popular central defenders the club has ever had, who played over 300 first team games between September 1989 and May 1995, was almost always referred to by his nickname – Chopper. His real name? Mark Harris.

Fact: obviously, in the club's first ever match, against Cardiff City on 7 September 1912, all 11 players were making their Swansea Town debuts. But only one would have the honour of being the first Swans player to score a debut goal, doing so in the 1–1 draw. The name of this history maker? Billy Ball.

Questions

1. John Toshack made his debut for the club on 3 March 1978 and scored in a 3–3 draw. Who were the Swans' opponents at the Vetch that day?

2. Who was the goalkeeper who made his debut in his second spell at the club on 24 August 1983 against Magdeburg in the European Cup Winners Cup, just under ten years after he made his first in November 1973?

3. Who was the Scottish centre back who had a baptism of fire on his Swans debut, making it in the 1–0 home defeat against Cardiff City at the Vetch on Boxing Day 1989?

4. Which 19-year-old midfielder, who had signed for the club from Llanelli, made his league debut away at Port Vale on 16 April 2001? He made 62 league appearances, scoring six goals for the Swans before being released by Brian Flynn at the end of the 2002/03 season.

5. Which striker scored on his League debut for the club, after 82 minutes of the 4–2 home win over Bury on 9 August 2003?

6. Who was the future manager of the club, who made his playing debut on 7 August 2004 in a 2–0 home defeat against Northampton Town?

7. Which 17-year-old midfielder made his league debut for the club on the final day of the 2006/07 season, in the incredible 6–3 home defeat to Blackpool?

8. Can you name the Spanish player who made his debut for the club as a 66th minute substitute for Jason Scotland on 16 August 2008, scoring the third goal against Nottingham Forest just 20 minutes after being introduced?

9. Which three players made their full debuts (not as substitutes) for the club in the first Premier League game away at Manchester City, in the 4–0 defeat on 15 August 2011?

10. Wilfried Bony and Jordi Amat both made their full Swans debuts in the Europa League third qualifying round, first leg, at home against Malmö on 1 August 2013. But which other player also made his first full appearance for the club in that game?

Did you know?

On 18 October 1930, Dai 'Jinky' Lewis made his debut as an amateur for the Swans away in a 2–2 draw at Burnley. The following season, now a professional and playing 39 of a possible 42 league games, he was credited with creating the bulk of Cyril Pearce's record-breaking 35 league goals.

Answers

1. Watford.
2. Jimmy Rimmer.
3. Keith Walker.
4. Andrew Mumford.
5. Lee Trundle.
6. Garry Monk.
7. Joe Allen.
8. Gorka Pintado.
9. Michel Vorm, Steven Caulker and Danny Graham.
10. Jonjo Shelvey.

The 1970s

Fact: the 1973/74 season was one of the worst Cup seasons in the club's history. They were knocked out in the first round of both the FA and the Football League cups by Walsall and Exeter City respectively, and then in their first game of the Welsh Cup, they were beaten 2–1 at home by non-league Stourbridge.

Questions

1. What specifically happened to the club at midnight on 24 February 1970?

2. In July 1970, the Swans broke their transfer record when they signed Swansea boy Barrie Hole for £20,000. But from which giants of the English game was he signed?

3. On 23 January 1971, the Swans travelled to Anfield in the fourth round of the FA Cup, losing 3–0. But which of the four future Swans in the Liverpool line-up scored Liverpool's opener?

4. On 25 August 1972 at Southend, two Swans youngsters made their league debuts. One was Mickey Lenihan, but who was the other, who was replaced by Dai Gwyther after 63 minutes?

5. Which former Liverpool player, who had made 94 league appearances for the Swans in the late 1950s and early 1960s acted as caretaker manager from 16 October to 25 November 1972, following Roy Bentley's resignation?

6. In the early 1970s, the Screen brothers – Tony and Willie – were regular members of the first team, both making over 100 league appearances for the club. Which of the two played in the most league games for the club – 142 against 128?

7. What was sold by the club for £50,000 in December 1974?

8. Which manager resigned his position on 23 January 1975, the season the club finished in the bottom four of the Fourth Division, meaning they had to embarrassingly apply for re-election to the Football League?

9. In March 1976, which Swansea City player was picked to play for Wales for the first time since a previous Swans player was picked in May 1973?

10. Who was that winger picked for Wales back in May 1973?

Did you know?
In the summer of 1976, the Vetch hosted a sell-out concert featuring one of the world's biggest bands, The Who. Just weeks later, in the September, the club were told that the Vetch no longer met the standards to host international football matches.

Answers

1. Swansea Town officially became known as Swansea City.
2. Aston Villa.
3. John Toshack.
4. Alan Curtis.
5. Roy Saunders.
6. Willie Screen.
7. The Vetch Field (to the Council).
8. Harry Gregg.
9. Alan Curtis.
10. Brian Evans.

Anagrams

The following are all anagrams of goalkeepers who have
played at least 25 games for Swansea City.

1. Disused Rover

2. Go Snort Referee!

3. Lord Weeny

4. Unforced Gift Gong

5. Hmm ... I Clover

6. I'd Advise A ...

7. Mart Held Merger

8. Twit Dad Raves

9. Treetops Vet

10. Ugly Were Lit

Did you know?

Between 1988 and 1992, 'Cereal Bye' was a young keeper who made 99 league appearances after having signed for the Swans from West Ham Utd as a 19- year-old.

The 1980s

Fact: most Swans fans will know that footballing giants Leeds United were thrashed 5–1 in the opening game of the club's first ever season in the top flight in August 1981. But many may not remember that Leeds never really recovered from that first day humiliation at the Vetch, and along with Wolves and Middlesbrough, they were relegated at the end of the season.

Questions

1. Toshack signed Welsh international keeper Dai Davies in July 1981 for £45,000 from which club?

2. Toshack again broke the club's transfer record for the last time when he signed which defender from Liverpool in August 1981?

3. Unforgettably for all who witnessed it, the Swans beat Leeds 5–1 on that glorious opening day in the First Division, but what was the half-time score?

4. Who replaced Terry Medwin as the Swans' assistant manager for the 1981/82 season due to Medwin's ill-health?

5. In September 1981, Toshack bought midfielder Gary Stanley for £150,000. From which club?

6. Between 16 February and 20 March 1982, which record did keeper Dai Davies set, beating the previous record held jointly by Jack Parry and Tony Millington?

7. The Swans beat Cardiff in the final of the Welsh Cup in 1982, winning the second leg 2–1 after drawing the first 0–0 in Cardiff. Who scored both Swans goals?

8. Who was voted the Swans' Player of the Year in their first season in Division One?

9. Dai Davies played in every league game in the 1981/82 season apart from the last one, a 3–0 defeat at Aston Villa. Who was the keeper that day?

10. Which former England international played 18 league games in the 1981/82 season, scoring two goals?

Did you know?

In the Swans' first season in Division One, they finished in sixth place. In that same season, Cardiff and Wrexham were relegated to Division Three, joining Newport County, meaning Swansea were, proudly, Wales' leading club by some distance.

Answers

1. Wrexham.
2. Colin Irwin.
3. 1–1.
4. Phil Boersma.
5. Everton.
6. Keeping six consecutive clean sheets in the league.
7. Bob Latchford.
8. Robbie James.
9. Chris Sander.
10. Ray Kennedy.

Division One with Tosh
Season One 1981/82

Fact: *the Swans won 69 points in the league that season. The team that finished above them on 71 was Arsenal.*

Questions

1. On 10 October the Swans beat Arsenal 2–0 at the Vetch. Who was the former Liverpool centre half with the Christian name Max, who scored with a spectacular volley direct from a corner?

2. That season, Swansea were knocked out at the first hurdle of the FA Cup, losing 0–4 in the third round at the Vetch. Which team beat them?

3. What was the name of the Yugoslavian (now Bosnian) central defender whom many critics hailed as the best central defender in the division?

4. Who was the Swans' kit manufacturer in that first season?

   (Note: There was no shirt advertising sponsor.)

5. Which team attracted the lowest home league attendance at the Vetch, just 11,811? Was it Notts County, Stoke City or Coventry City?

6. Which distinction did Notts County, Sunderland, Arsenal and Stoke City share in relation to the Swans during the season?

7. The Swans were knocked out of the European Cup Winners' Cup in the first round by an East German team 3–1 on aggregate. Can you name the team?

8. Nearly every Swans fan knows that the first league game that season was the 5–1 victory over Leeds United at home. But what was the score in the return fixture at Elland Road on 16 January 1982?

9. Only two players scored over ten league goals that season. One scored fifteen, the other twelve. Can you name them?

10. The Swans finished sixth in that first season in the top division, but which current mid-table Premier League team finished three points behind the Swans in seventh place?

Did you know?

Swansea City beat Aston Villa 2–1 at the Vetch that season, with goals from Robbie James. At the end of the season, Aston Villa won the European Cup.

Answers

1. Max Thompson.
2. Liverpool.
3. Ante Rajkovic.
4. Patrick.
5. Stoke City.
6. They were the teams the Swans did the double over (beat them at home and away).
7. Lokomotive Leipzig.
8. 2–0 to Leeds.
9. Robbie James (15), Bob Latchford (12).
10. Southampton.

The Premier League Season One 2011/12

Fact: *the lowest home attendance of the season at the Liberty Stadium was 18,985 for the visit by Blackburn Rovers on 14 April 2012.*

Questions

1. In terms of the history of the Premier League, what was unique about the Swans' home match against Wigan Athletic?

2. Which nationality was loan signing Gylfi Sigurdsson?

3. Which player provided most goal assists for the club in the Premier League with seven?

4. Gerhard Tremmel made one league appearance when Michel Vorm was taken ill on the morning of an away game. Against whom?

5. What was significant about the opening goal scored by Andrea Orlandi against Wolverhampton Wanderers at the Liberty on 28 April 2012?

6. Which squad number was worn by Leroy Lita during the season?

7. From which club did the Swans loan Steven Caulker?

8. Which player was loaned to Blackpool during the season?

9. Danny Graham scored the most league goals throughout the season with 12, but who scored the next highest amount with eight?

10. Which three players captained the club in Premier League games during the season?

Did you know?
The Swans had only one South American player in their squad in the first Premier League season, the Argentine Fede Bessone.

Ivor

Fact: *Ivor Allchurch actually played for another club before making his debut for the Swans. While he was serving as a gunner in the Army, based at Oswestry during his national service, he made an appearance for Shrewsbury Town in the Welsh Cup against Lovells Athletic in January 1949, almost a full year before taking his Swans bow on Boxing Day 1949.*

Questions

1. In which year did Ivor sign for the club as a teenager, having been spotted by former Swans legend Joe Sykes, playing in an Under-16s match, quickly followed by an Under-18s match at Cwm Level on the same afternoon?

2. Ivor made his first team debut for the Swans in an away Division Two match on Boxing Day 1949. But which London club spoiled Ivor's debut by winning the game 3–0?

3. Against which country did Ivor make his full Wales debut on 15 November 1950 in the Home Internationals or British Championship of the 1950/51 season?

4. The 1953/54 season was the first one that Ivor, then 24, finished as the club's top scorer in the league. In his 40 league appearances that year, how many goals did he score?

5. In his eight full seasons with the Swans, prior to leaving in 1958, how many times did Ivor finish as the club's top league goalscorer for the season?

6. Which club paid their club record transfer of £28,000 plus player Reg Davies for Ivor's services in October 1958?

7. Ivor returned to the club in July 1965, signed by then manager Glyn Davies for £6,500. But from which club did Ivor rejoin the Swans?

8. Ivor last played for Wales in May 1966, less than five months before his 37th birthday, and after a season in which the Swans finished 17th in Division Three. That final appearance was away in Chile, but what did it take Ivor's final Welsh cap total for Wales to?

9. Ivor's record for appearances made for Wales whilst a Swansea player was 42 caps, which stood until the 2013/14 season. Which Swans player passed Ivor's mark when he won his 44th cap, which was his 43rd whilst a Swans player?

10. Ivor made 445 league appearances for the club in his two spells. How many league goals did he score for the Swans?

Did you know?
When Ivor finally left the Swans in 1958, the deal was for a reported £28,000 plus another player, Reg Davies, making the deal an approximate £33,000 in total. To give that transfer some modern context, the value of £33,000 in 1958 in today's money is approximately £660,000, clearly an enormous amount of money in post-war Britain, and one of the highest ever value transfers in British football at that time.

Answers

1. 1947.
2. West Ham United.
3. England.
4. 17.
5. Three (he was also runner-up three times).
6. Newcastle United.
7. Cardiff City.
8. 68.
9. Ashley Williams.
10. 164.

The 1980s

Fact: *when the club sacked the manager in December 1984, they appointed Les Chappell as caretaker. When the club announced that they were intent on bringing in a big name, Chappell felt aggrieved and left when the new manager arrived.*

Questions

1. Who was appointed manager for the start of the 1984/85 season?

2. In the first home game of the season against York City on 1 September 1984, which future Championship winner in a different professional sport was given his debut?

3. During October 1984, another former England captain briefly joined the club, making his debut against Walsall in a 2–1 home defeat. Who was he?

4. Due to an awful start to the season, when 12 games of the first 18 in the league were lost, the manager was sacked. Who was brought in as his full time replacement on 16 December 1984?

5. Before the final match of the season, the Swans lay on 46 points, in the relegation zone below Leyton Orient and Burnley. However, those two clubs had played their final games, meaning a Swans draw at home would deliver safety. They managed it with a 0–0 draw, but against whom?

6. Who was the Swans keeper who delivered an astonishing performance in that vital relegation-saving 0–0 draw?

7. Which 37-year-old winger joined the club from Burnley for the 1985/86 season?

8. Dean Saunders was allowed to leave the club on a free transfer in August 1985. Who did he join?

9. Despite another relegation season, the Swans managed a 5–1 victory in an away match on 14 September 1985. Which once-great club did they beat?

10. In which league position did the Swans finish the 1985/86 season?

Did you know?

During the 1984/85 season, when relegation from Division Three was only avoided by a 0–0 draw in the final game, the three managers of the club used an astonishing 39 players during the season, the most since 41 were used in the first season after World War Two.

Answers

1. Colin Appleton.
2. Tony Cottey.
3. Gerry Francis.
4. John Bond.
5. Bristol City.
6. Jimmy Rimmer.
7. Tommy Hutchison.
8. Brighton and Hove Albion.
9. Wolverhampton Wanderers.
10. Bottom (24th).

Managers as players

Can you recognise the managers of the Swans from details of their own playing careers given below?

1. Made his Chelsea debut in 1963 aged 17, went on to make 436 league appearances for them before re-joining them after 151 league games for QPR and 127 for Arsenal. Played once for England, against Spain in 1967.

2. Signed for Wolves in May 1936, but moved on to Swindon Town without playing a league game for Wolves. After 144 games for the Robins, he joined the Swans in 1948 for £11,000, playing 205 league games before joining Newport in 1953. Won seven full caps for Wales.

3. A goalkeeper, he played for Doncaster Rovers, Manchester United and Stoke City and also played 25 times for Northern Ireland, including at the 1958 World Cup. He retired in 1967.

4. Started his career at Kolding, played 57 times for Ajax before playing for Liverpool, Barnsley and Norwich City. Played 41 league games for Swansea.

5. A 13-times capped Welsh international defender, he began at QPR in 1970 before playing 137 league games for Crystal Palace and 102 for Barnsley. Retired in 1984.

6. Played one game for Ipswich Town on the last day of the 1938/39 season, with World War Two meaning he never played league football again. Managed Cardiff City for four seasons before joining the Swans.

7. Came south from Raith Rovers to Scunthorpe in 1965, making 106 league appearances for the Iron before moving to Swindon Town. Over 300 appearances later, he retired in 1976. Also played six games on loan to Mansfield Town, before taking up his first managerial position at Portsmouth in 1979.

8. Made 87 league appearances for York City before another 160 at Nottingham Forest between 1961 and 1966. Twenty-eight games at Arsenal followed, before he joined Sheffield United in 1967. Ended his career after 44 league games for Hereford in 1973, where he'd been appointed player-manager in 1971.

9. Began at Leicester City in 1987, moved to Peterborough United and then north to Motherwell in 1989 for three seasons and 77 games. Moves to Darlington, Oxford and Fulham followed, before playing over 200 matches for the Swans.

10. Won 66 caps for Wales in a career with Burnley, Leeds United, Cardiff, Doncaster, Bury, and ended his career at Wrexham. Played over 550 league games.

A to Z – the letter G

All the answers in this quiz are surnames of former
Swans players beginning with the letter G.

Questions

1. Dubbed the 'new Kevin Keegan', this busy striker
   scored 13 goals in 54 league games before being
   sold to Crystal Palace in 1982. Also played for
   Cardiff, Wrexham and Newport along with 12
   games for Wales.

2. Joined Swans ground staff from South Gower in
   1964. A big striker, he scored 60 league goals for
   Swans before joining Halifax in 1973. Scored a hat-
   trick for Rotherham against Swans at the Vetch in
   legendary 4–4 draw in 1978.

3. Peter, the former Spurs keeper who only played
   14 games on loan for the Swans in 1988, but they
   included the victorious 1987/88 Fourth Division
   play-offs.

4. League debut 1950. 421 league appearances.
   72 goals. One Welsh cap. Chief scout, trainer,
   physiotherapist, coach, assistant manager, manager.
   Legend.

5. Originally signed on loan during League Two
   season of 2004/05, signed permanently for League
   One the following season. A pacey, wide player,
   he only scored three goals, but is remembered for
   scoring first ever goal at Liberty Stadium.

6. Tough-tackling full back signed from Manchester
   City in 1966. Played over 200 times for the club,
   finishing up working in the Swans' commercial
   department for many years, and also the match day
   announcer at the Vetch.

7. Popular former Cardiff striker, signed from Portsmouth in 1990. Top scorer with 16 league goals in first season. In December 1990, he scored eight goals in four Swans matches. His career was ended by a serious back injury.

8. Young, powerful, pacey, Port Talbot-born striker, a broken leg cut short his career. Played 37 league games between 1982 and 1985 and scored in Division One during Swans' relegation season. Joined Exeter in 1985. Retired in 1986.

9. Imposing keeper signed from Millwall in 2004. Was arrested at Bury during celebrations for promotion from League Two. Made 135 league appearances for the Swans before making a similar number for MK Dons.

10. Much-travelled striker who scored 15 league goals for the Swans in 54 games. Not including his many loan clubs, his other teams have been Middlesbrough, Carlisle United, Watford and Sunderland. Still playing.

Miscellaneous

> **Fact:** in 1961, the club made a young player their first ever apprentice professional. The lucky young footballer was Denis Lambourne.

Questions

1. Which player, who would go on to play over 100 times for England and come runner-up to Ronaldinho in the 2005 Ballon d'Or, made his Swans debut against Bradford City ten years earlier?

2. In April 1936 the Swans set a record for the number of miles travelled between two consecutive games when they played on Good Friday and Easter Saturday. They played Plymouth on the Friday. Where did they play on the Saturday?

3. When Wales played Northern Ireland in Belfast on 15 April 1953, all five of the attacking players picked by Wales were born in Swansea. Can you name them?

4. In the 1953/54 season, three sets of brothers played for the Swans. One set was the Allchurch brothers. Who were the other two sets?

5. What was strange about goalkeeper John King's appearance against Rotherham away in September 1956?

6. In the 1960/61 season, floodlights were erected at the Vetch for the first time. Which Scottish team came to play the Swans in the match to officially open the lights?

7. During the 1980/81 season, which Welsh international rugby union player signed as a non-contract player for the Swans, having also previously signed as a 16-year-old schoolboy? He never made a first team appearance.

8. Up to and including the 2014/15 season, who is the Vice Chairman of Swansea City?

9. Which midfielder, who made 19 league appearances in the early 1980s for the Swans, is now the club's Player Liaison Officer?

10. Former Swans striker John Hughes is currently manager of which Scottish Premiership Club?

Did you know?
The Swans were the first ever Welsh club to compete in a European competition.

Answers

1. Frank Lampard.
2. Newcastle United.
3. John Charles, Trevor Ford, Terry Medwin, Harry Griffiths and Ivor Allchurch.
4. The Beech brothers and the Jones brothers.
5. He started and played the whole game at centre forward.
6. Hibernian.
7. Gareth Edwards.
8. Leigh Dineen.
9. Huw Lake.
10. Inverness Caledonian Thistle.

The 1990s

Fact: *when the Swans sold Chris Coleman to Crystal Palace in 1991, the fee was settled by a tribunal. The Swans wanted £500,000 and Palace offered £175,000. The result? £275,000, but with additional bonuses linked to league appearances, and a sell-on clause.*

Questions

1. Fans' favourite and future captain John Cornforth joined the Swans for the start of the 1991/92 season from which club?

2. Frank Burrows signed two players from the same non-league club in 1991, who would both give good service to the Swans, for the bargain price of £5,000 each. One was John Williams. Who was the other?

3. From which non-league club were both players signed?

4. Who was the classy midfielder signed on loan from Oxford United in October 1991, who made a big impact in a short spell at the club, eventually leaving Oxford for West Ham United in a £1 million deal?

5. Which top division side did the Swans beat 1–0 in the first leg of the Rumbelows Cup in September 1991 with a goal from Jimmy Gilligan?

6. Who did the Swans knock out of the FA Cup on 16 November 1991, beating them 2–1 at the Vetch with goals from Gilligan and Harris?

7. Three players scored hat-tricks in Division Three football for the Swans in the 1991/92 season. Jimmy Gilligan was one, who were the other two? One was a striker, the other a left-sided midfielder.

8. After just one season with the club, Burrows cashed in on the bargain £5,000 he paid for John Williams by selling him for a reported £250,000, but to which club?

9. Burrows replaced Williams by giving £20,000 to Portsmouth for another striker, originally from the same non-league team as Williams. Who was he?

10. Which two players were the mainstay of the club's central defence in the 1992/93 season, both playing 42 of the 46 league matches?

Did you know?
The only visit to the Vetch Field by a royal head of state was on 17 September 1991, when Prince Rainier came to watch his Monaco team in the European Cup Winners' Cup.

Strikers

Fact: *Carl Heggs was signed for £60,000 from Bristol Rovers in 1995, with high hopes, but he was never prolific, scoring just seven goals in 46 league appearances before leaving for Northampton Town in 1997 for £40,000.*

Questions

1. Jimmy Gilligan scored 23 league goals in 62 appearances in a Swans career beset by injury. From which club did the Swans sign him in August 1990?

2. Which Swans striker scored 60 goals in 216 league appearances from 1965 to 1973, but is also remembered for scoring a hat-trick against the Swans for Rotherham in September 1978 in a thrilling 4–4 draw at the Vetch?

3. Who was the former Millwall trainee that the Swans signed from Bradford in 1993, and went on to score 44 league goals for the club before joining Bristol City in 1997 for £400,000?

4. Dean Saunders was released by John Bond and went on to enjoy a stellar playing career. How many goals did he score for Wales in his 75 games?

5. Which veteran striker with the Christian name Stan was signed by the Swans from Cardiff in 1948? He contributed an amazing 26 league goals in just 32 games in the Third Division (South) Championship winning season of 1948/49.

6. Cyril Pearce holds the Swans' record for the highest number of league goals scored in one season with 35, but in how many games did he score the goals?

7. Des Palmer scored 38 league goals in 84 games between 1952 and 1959, but to which of the giant clubs of north-west England was he sold in 1959 for £4,000?

8. Who was the striker signed from Portsmouth in 1992 for £20,000, who scored eight goals in 55 league appearances before being sold to Scunthorpe in 1995?

9. Which striker scored an incredible 102 goals in 167 league appearances for Swansea Town between 1924 and 1930?

10. Who scored 72 goals in 314 games for the Swans in all football between 1976 and 1984 before moving to QPR?

Did you know?

Arguably the finest striker to play for the Swans only played 16 official games for the club due to the war, scoring nine goals. His name was Trevor Ford.

Answers

1. Portsmouth.
2. David Gwyther.
3. Steve Torpey.
4. 22.
5. Stan Richards.
6. 40.
7. Liverpool.
8. Andy McFarlane.
9. Jack Fowler.
10. Jeremy Charles.

The south Wales derby

Fact: Ivor Allchurch appeared in 17 south Wales derbies, playing for both Swansea and Cardiff. However, it could have been 18, because he was handed his Swans debut on 26 December 1949, just two days after the Swans beat Cardiff 5–1.

Questions

1. True or false? Cardiff have beaten Swansea more times than Swansea have beaten them in the League Cup.

2. Which future Swans manager scored Cardiff's two goals in Cardiff's 2–1 League Cup win at Ninian Park on 20 August 1985?

3. The last time the derby took place in the League Cup was at the Liberty on 23 September 2008, when the Swans won 1–0. But which on-loan midfielder scored the Swans' goal from a free kick?

4. In April 2009 the derby was drawn 2–2 in an extremely controversial match in which the referee was hit by a coin. What was the ref's name?

5. The game played earlier in that 2008/09 season was also a 2–2 draw, at the Liberty. Which Swans player scored the equaliser three minutes after coming on as sub?

6. In that same 2–2 draw, which Swans player was sent off in the 90th minute?

7. Who scored five derby goals for Cardiff between August 1987 and December 1989, then scored for the Swans against Cardiff in a 2–1 FA Cup win in November 1991?

8. In 1962, the two derby league games were played within ten days of each other, with both clubs winning one each. Which Swansea-born player scored for Cardiff in both games, a total of three goals?

9. The first derby was played in 1912. Who scored the Swans' first ever goal in the match in the 1–1 draw?

10. What was the score of the last ever derby played at the Vetch in November 1998?

Did you know?

In total, there have been 107 derby matches in all competitions (not including wartime games or the South Wales & Monmouthshire Cup), and Cardiff have won 44 to Swansea's 36. But if Welsh Cup games are ignored, it reads Cardiff 23, Swansea 29. In league football, 56 matches have now been played, with Swansea winning 21 and Cardiff nineteen.

Answers

1. False – there have been five matches and the Swans have won three.
2. Brian Flynn.
3. Jordi Gómez.
4. Mike Dean.
5. Gorka Pintado
6. Leon Britton.
7. Jimmy Gilligan.
8. John Charles.
9. Billy Ball.
10. 2–1 to Swansea.

93

Firsts

Fact: *the first ever match the club played in European competition was in October 1961 against East German team Motor Jena. The result was a 2–2 draw, with Swansea's goals coming from Brayley Reynolds and captain Mel Nurse's penalty.*

Questions

1. In 1924, against Charlton Athletic, who became the first, and as yet only, player to score five goals in Football League match for the Swans?

2. What was the first honour ever won by the Swans after forming in 1912?

3. Who was the first player to cost Swansea City over £5 million?

4. Who was the first player to score over 150 league goals for the club?

5. Who was the first player to be sold by the club for at least £1 million?

6. On 14 February 1920, Ivor Jones became the first player from the Swans to do what?

7. Who were Swansea City's opponents in their first competitive match at the Liberty Stadium on 23 July 2005 in a testimonial game for Alan Curtis?

8. Which team did the Swans play in their first ever home Premier League match on 20 August 2011?

9. In 1982, which Maltese team became the first team that Swansea City scored more than ten goals against in a competitive match?

10. Which player scored the first Premier League goal for the Swans in the reign of Michael Laudrup?

Did you know?

The first club the Swans ever played in the Football League proper was Portsmouth away in their first Third Division match on 28 August 1920. The Swans lost 3–0 on the day. Their first league win came five days later, beating Watford 2–1 at the Vetch, with the winning goal coming from Ivor Jones.

Answers

1. Jack Fowler.
2. The Welsh Cup.
3. Ki Sung-yueng (the week before Pablo Hernández).
4. Ivor Allchurch.
5. Lee Trundle.
6. Play for Wales.
7. Fulham.
8. Wigan Athletic.
9. Sliema Wanderers.
10. Michu.

The 1990s

> **Fact:** in the 1995/96 relegation season, 18-year-old Kristian O'Leary made his debut appearance against Bradford City away, the first of over 300 first team games he played for the Swans. Another player, striker Lee Chapman, also made his Swans debut in the same game, but he was only to make six further league appearances before moving on.

Questions

1. In the 1994/95 FA Cup, which Division One club (not Premier League) did the Swans knock out in a third-round replay away from home after drawing the first game 1–1 at the Vetch?

2. Who was the Welsh international winger-cum-striker who left the Vetch on 24 July 1995 for Birmingham City in a reported £350,000 deal, following over 150 first team games and 39 goals?

3. Who was the striker the Swans signed three days after the above departure in a £60,000 deal from West Bromwich Albion?

4. Who was the manager who resigned his post in October 1995 after over 200 games in charge since his appointment in 1991?

5. And who was the manager who replaced the above manager – initially on a caretaker basis – who only lasted until December 1995?

6. Which midfielder arrived at the club on loan on 6 October 1995, scoring his first ever goal in English league football before returning to his

parent club after nine league games and that
solitary goal, to carry out the rest of what became
a distinguished career?

7. Which club humiliated the Swans in the FA Cup in
November 1995 by beating them 7–0 away from
the Vetch?

8. In December 1995, which player's transfer from
Crystal Palace to Blackburn Rovers netted the
Swans £800,000 in a sell-on clause?

9. Who provided the opposition for the only home
game in the (thankfully) short reign of Kevin Cullis
in February 1996?

10. Who was appointed permanent manager eight days
after Cullis was dismissed?

Did you know?
*When Doug Sharpe sold the club to Michael Thompson
and subsequently heard of Kevin Cullis' appointment, he
flew back from holiday immediately to cancel the deal
in the 21-day cooling-off contract period.*

Answers

1. Middlesbrough.
2. Jason Bowen.
3. Carl Heggs.
4. Frank Burrows.
5. Bobby Smith.
6. Frank Lampard.
7. Fulham.
8. Chris Coleman.
9. Swindon Town.
10. Jan Molby.

Can you recognise the Swans player below from the clubs that have made up their careers? The dates relate to their career span and an asterisk (*) denotes a loan spell.

1. 2002 – present: Tranmere Rovers, Swansea City, Leeds United, Tranmere Rovers, Shrewsbury Town.

2. 1985–2001: Sunderland, Doncaster Rovers*, Shrewsbury Town*, Lincoln City*, Swansea City, Birmingham City, Wycombe Wanderers, Peterborough United*, Cardiff City, Scunthorpe United, Exeter City.

3. 1999 – present: Telstar, ADO Den Haag, Dunfermline Athletic, Swansea City, Wolverhampton Wanderers, Nottingham Forest.

4. 1986–2004: Newport County, Chelsea, Swansea City*, Hereford United*, Swansea City, Newport County.

5. 1965–1991: Alloa Athletic, Blackpool, Coventry City, Seattle Sounders*, Manchester City, Bulova, Burnley, Swansea City.

6. 1980–1993: Swansea City, Huddersfield Town, Halifax Town*, Wrexham, Halifax Town, Torquay United.

7. 1965–1983: Crewe Alexandra, Stoke City, Middlesbrough, Swansea City.

8. 1990–2004. Cradley Town, Swansea City, Coventry City, Notts County*, Stoke City*, Swansea City*, Wycombe Wanderers, Hereford United, Walsall, Exeter City, Cardiff City, York City, Darlington, Swansea City, Kidderminster Harriers.

9. 1993–2007: Real Zaragoza, Balaguer, Wigan Athletic, Motherwell, Walsall, Swansea City, Chester City.

10. 2005 – present: Hapoel Nazareth Illit, Maccabi Netanya, Hapoel Tel Aviv, FC Kaiserslautern, Swansea City*, Hapoel Tel Aviv, Nantes.

Did you know?
Terry Medwin only played for two clubs – Swansea and Tottenham Hotspur – making 344 league appearances in total before a broken leg ended his career at just 31 years of age.

Answers

1. Andy Robinson.
2. John Cornforth.
3. Dorus de Vries.
4. Roger Freestone.
5. Tommy Hutchison.
6. Dudley Lewis.
7. John Mahoney.
8. John Williams.
9. Roberto Martinez.
10. Itay Shechter.

European campaigns

Fact: *the manager of the Swans at the time of the 6–5 aggregate defeat by Panathinaikos in the 1989/90 European Cup Winners' Cup, is often incorrectly thought to have been Terry Yorath, but it was in fact Ian Evans.*

Questions

1. Who was the Swansea-born striker who scored the Swans' consolation goal in their 2–1 away defeat to Lokomotive Leipzig in September 1981?

2. Which Portuguese team did the Swans play in the preliminary round of the 1982/83 Cup Winners' Cup, beating them 3–1 on aggregate?

3. In the second leg of that preliminary round tie away in Portugal, which young Swansea-born full back scored an own goal for Braga?

4. In the first round proper of the 1982/83 campaign, Swansea beat Sliema Wanderers 12–0. Which striker scored a hat-trick in 11 minutes that night for the Swans, after coming on as 68th minute sub?

5. In that 12–0 victory, two other strikers scored two goals each. One had played since Division Four days, the other was a novice. Can you name them?

6. In the away leg against Sliema, a veteran striker who had hardly played for the club in the previous three seasons came off the bench to score the fifth and final goal. Who was he?

7. In the next round of that 1982/83 campaign, the Swans were drawn against Paris St Germain. Which Argentinian international, who had played at the Vetch Field before, played for PSG in midfield?

8. In 1989/90, the Swans had an incredible result away to Panathinaikos, narrowly losing 3–2. But which two strikers (one on loan) scored the Swans' goals?

9. In 1991/92, the Swans were knocked out 10–1 on aggregate by Monaco. But who was Monaco's manager over the two ties?

10. The first game the Swans played in Europe for 22 years, on 1 August 2013, was won 4–0. Who scored their first goal back on the European stage?

Did you know?

In the 10–1 aggregate defeat by Monaco in 1991/92, two goals were scored by a future African Player of the Year, European Player of the Year and World Player of the Year. His name? George Weah.

Answers

1. Jeremy Charles.
2. Sporting Braga.
3. Chris Marustik.
4. Ian Walsh.
5. Jeremy Charles and Jimmy Loveridge.
6. John Toshack.
7. Osvaldo Ardiles.
8. Paul Rayner and John Salako.
9. Arsène Wenger.
10. Michu.

Picture Quiz Three

Can you name all these players? Answers on p. 153

1.

2.

3.

4.

5.

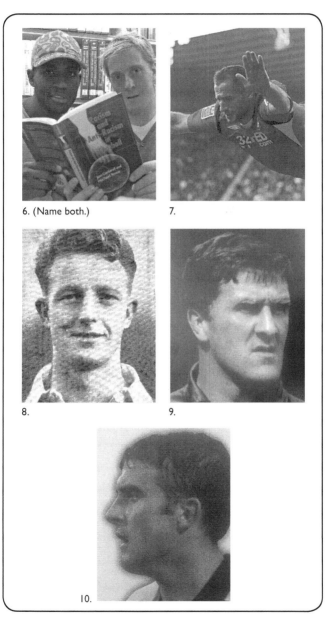

6. (Name both.)

7.

8.

9.

10.

Former players still playing

Below is a list of facts relating to players still playing football at the start of the 2014/15 season, who at some point in the past played league football for the Swans. Can you name them from those facts and the club they currently play for?

1. I signed for the Swans as a midfielder in September 2007 and, after scoring three league goals in 72 appearances, I joined Brighton and Hove Albion for the 2012/13 season. After 6 goals in 49 appearances, I signed for Blackpool in August 2014.

2. I signed for the Swans in a £600,000 deal from Sheffield United in 2009 before leaving for Barnsley in 2012. I left Barnsley for Doncaster Rovers, but I now play for Birmingham City.

3. After signing for Swansea on 1 August 2008, I never really managed to hold down a regular place, making 48 of my 73 league appearances from the bench. I was released in 2011 and joined AEK Larnaca in Greece, who I still play for.

4. I left Swansea in June 2011 on a free after 178 league games. Since then, I have started just 15 league matches up to 1 August 2014. I'm now at Nottingham Forest.

5. I joined the club in July 2008 from Espanyol for £80,000, but never settled properly so left in May 2011 after just 30 league appearances. I have now returned to Spain and play for Alcorcon in the Spanish Second Division.

6. I left the Swans in August 2013 after joining in January 2011, and joined Elazığspor in Turkey for the start of the 2013/14 season. However, in February 2014 I left Turkey for the MLS, joining Chivas USA.

I have since moved on to another MLS club, Toronto FC.

7. A local product, I had four separate loan spells away from the Swans with Yeovil Town before signing for my current club, Bournemouth, in August 2011.

8. I played for the Swans between June 2006 and July 2011 before joining Premier League Bolton. I am still with Bolton, but now in the Championship.

9. I had one of the shortest Swans careers ever, just four minutes in the game when the Swans conceded two late goals against Wolves away in the first Premier League season. A Greece international, I now play for Verona in Italy's Serie A.

10. I spent five seasons at Swansea after joining from Southend United, but left in June 2013 to join Charlton Athletic. I am now a free agent after being released by Charlton in May 2014.

Did you know?
Since leaving the Swans in January 2007 in a big money deal to Plymouth Argyle, striker Rory Fallon has had a further five different clubs, namely, Ipswich Town, Yeovil, Aberdeen, St Johnstone and Crawley Town. After joining Crawley in February 2014 on a free transfer, he was released at the end of the season and is now a free agent.

Answers

1. Andrea Orlandi.
2. David Cotterill.
3. Gorka Pintado.
4. Dorus de Vries.
5. Albert Serran.
6. Luke Moore.
7. Shaun MacDonald.
8. Darren Pratley.
9. Vangelis Moras.
10. Mark Gower.

Welsh internationals

Can you recognise the players who have represented Wales whilst playing for the Swans from details of their Welsh international careers? NB They may have also represented other clubs whilst playing for Wales, not just Swansea.

1. Three caps between December 1964 and November 1971. First cap v Greece, final cap v Romania. Won all three caps whilst playing for the Swans.

2. Eleven caps between April 1955 and December 1963. First cap v Northern Ireland, final cap v England. Won seven caps playing for the Swans, and four whilst with Sheffield United.

3. Two caps between May 1994 and November 1996. First cap v Estonia, final cap v Holland. Won first cap with the Swans, last one with Birmingham City.

4. Nineteen caps and one goal (the winner against Bulgaria) between November 1980 and September 1986. First cap v Czechoslovakia, final cap v Finland. Won first cap playing for the Swans, last one with Oxford United.

5. Forty caps and 13 goals between March 1969 and October 1979. First and last caps won v West Germany. Scored a hat-trick against Scotland in 1979 whilst with Swansea. Won his last six caps as a Swans player.

6. Goalkeeper, won 21 caps between October 1962 and November 1971. First cap v Scotland and the last v Romania. He won his caps representing four clubs – West Bromwich Albion, Crystal Palace and Peterborough United – and his final eight as a Swans player.

7. Thirty caps and six goals between April 1953 and November 1962. First cap, whilst with the Swans, was v Northern Ireland, last cap, whilst with Spurs, was v England. Played in 1958 World Cup.

8. Welsh one-cap wonder, making only appearance against Brazil at the Millennium Stadium in 2000 as a Swansea City player. Wales lost 3–0.

9. Six caps and three goals, reflecting his usual goalscoring ratio with the Swans, this centre forward won first cap v England in 1925 and final cap also against England in 1928. Won all caps as a Swansea Town player.

10. Sixty-eight caps scoring 23 goals, with first cap v England in 1950, last v Chile whilst back at Swansea, having won other caps whilst at Newcastle and Cardiff. Won 42 caps as a Swans player.

Did you know?

The first time that more than one Swans player represented Wales in a full international was when Billy Hole was picked for his debut alongside team mate Ivor Jones (winning his fourth cap) in the British Home Championship at the Vetch on 9 April 1921. Over 20,000 turned up to watch the Swans duo, in what was a personal triumph for the much-loved Hole, scoring the first goal in a 2–1 victory over Northern Ireland.

Answers

1. Herbie Williams.
2. Len Allchurch.
3. Jason Bowen.
4. Jeremy Charles.
5. John Toshack.
6. Tony Millington.
7. Terry Medwin.
8. Roger Freestone.
9. Jack Fowler.
10. Ivor Allchurch.

A to Z – the letter B

All the answers in this quiz are surnames of former Swans players beginning with the letter B.

Questions

1. Popular goalkeeper signed from Luton, played just one season – 1977/78 – and played in every league game. Surprisingly, Tosh replaced him with Geoff Crudgington; he was loaned to Cardiff and never played for the club again.

2. Merthyr-born winger, signed as a trainee in 1990 before scoring 26 league goals in 124 games. Sold to Birmingham in 1995 for £350,000. Won two Wales caps.

3. Born in Wimbledon in 1982, previously with Arsenal and West Ham and also Lilleshall Football Academy. First signed for Swans on loan in 2002. Legend.

4. Combative centre half, mainstay for the club during the mid-1970s. Played 192 league games after signing from Bristol City in 1973 before joining Newport County in 1978. Formed effective partnership with Eddie May and was a regular penalty taker.

5. Made 99 league appearances as a goalkeeper after being signed from West Ham in 1988 before moving to Halifax in 1991. Man of the Match v Liverpool in 0–0 FA Cup tie in January 1990.

6. Nicknamed 'The Pearl', this Jamaican international scored 10 league goals for Swans between 1999 and 2001. Once sent off for the Swans within 57 seconds of coming on.

7. Former Liverpool winger, signed from Luton in 1978, broke leg horrifically at Swindon in his 18th game and never played again. Became Tosh's assistant.

8. Extremely popular left-sided player, played 198 league games between 1973 and 1980. Lost his place to Chris Marustik and Dave Rushbury so joined Hereford.

9. Former Cardiff striker, signed from Barry Town by Jan Molby in 1997. Top scorer in 1997/98 season with 14 goals after scoring on Swans debut. Loaned to Merthyr in 1999, subsequently re-joined Molby at Kidderminster in 2000.

10. 'Frankie' was a real favourite in the 1940s, scoring eight goals in 171 league games between 1946 and 1952. A tough tackler, was an ever present in the Third Division South Championship win with Swans in 1948/49.

Did you know?
Life hasn't run smoothly for Craig Beattie since leaving the Swans. He has had five clubs since leaving the Liberty, the last of which, Dundee, released him at the end of the 2013/14 season, just a month after he declared himself bankrupt with debts of £70,000. In an effort to resurrect his career, in July 2014 he headed for India's 1–League and a trial with Salgaocar.

Answers

1. Keith Barber.
2. Jason Bowen.
3. Leon Britton.
4. Dave Bruton.
5. Lee Bracey.
6. Walter Boyd.
7. Phil Boersma.
8. Danny Bartley.
9. Tony Bird.
10. Frank 'Frankie' Burns.

Top scorers

Can you spot which of the Swans' players below
were the top league scorers in the given season, from
the number of goals scored and the players given as
options? NB Figures relate to League games only.

1. 2005/06   20 goals   Lee Trundle, Adebayo
Akinfenwa or Andy
Robinson?

2. 1957/58   14 goals   Mel Charles, Len Allchurch
or Ivor Allchurch?

3. 1983/84   6 goals   Ian Walsh, Bob Latchford or
Dean Saunders?

4. 2009/10   7 goals   Darren Pratley, Lee Trundle
or Shefki Kuqi?

5. 1990/91   16 goals   Paul Raynor, Terry Connor or
Jimmy Gilligan?

6. 1998/99   17 goals   Stuart Roberts, Steve Watkin
or Julian Alsop?

7. 1965/66   20 goals   Keith Todd, Ivor Allchurch or
Jimmy McLaughlin?

8. 2011/12   12 goals   Scott Sinclair, Gylfi Sigurdsson
or Danny Graham?

9. 1970/71   18 goals   Herbie Williams, David
Gwyther or Willie Screen?

10. 1934/35   11 goals   Tudor Martin, Sid Lowry or
Walter Bussey?

Did you know?

When Cyril Pearce set the Swans' record for goals scored in a league season with 35 goals in 40 games in the 1931/32 season, it was his first season with the club after scoring 22 goals in 27 games for Newport the season before. Then he left to join Charlton in the 1932/33 season. In 68 league games for Charlton, he scored an amazing 52 goals before ending his career with one last season with the Swans in 1937/38, scoring eight goals in 15 games – the worst season's goal-to-games ratio of his career! In total, this incredible striker scored 117 goals in 150 league games.

Fact: *in the 2001/02 season in League Division Three, which saw the Swans finish in twentieth position, just avoiding relegation, the Swans strangely scored more goals away from home than at the Vetch – 27 against 26.*

Questions

1. What was the nationality of David Romo, a player signed in October 2000 who made 43 league appearances before leaving the club in 2002?

2. In the first game of the 2001/02 season away at Macclesfield, the Swans won 3–1. On the bench that day was a midfielder called Nicolas Mazzina, who had impressed on trial. Which country was he from?

3. Who was the former Swansea City trainee who left the club in October 2001 in a deal worth over £100,000 after 96 league appearances and 14 goals? He returned to the club on loan for 12 games in February 2004, before moving on to Kidderminster Harriers.

4. Which Second Division team did Third Division Swansea knock out of the FA Cup in a 4–0 win at the Vetch in November 2001?

5. In the 2001/02 season, the Swans were beaten home and away by Hartlepool. They lost 1–0 at the Vetch, but what was the horror score away in Hartlepool?

6. Who was Roger Freestone's understudy, who left the club at the end of the 2001/02 season after making just ten league appearances in five seasons?

7. Toward the end of the 2001/02 season, Colin Addison left the club, but which two players were jointly appointed to replace him?

8. Who was appointed full-time manager in September 2002?

9. Which player, who had joined the club from school, was sadly forced to retire in January 2003 due to injury, aged just 25, after over 100 first team games?

10. Roberto Martínez had a big influence on the 2002/03 season after joining on 28 January 2003. But which club did he arrive from?

Did you know?
Most Swans fans know that James Thomas ended the 2002/03 season with the final goal in the crucial relegation game against Hull. But in the opening game of the season, also at the Vetch, he had scored the season's first goal after just 15 minutes against Rushden & Diamonds in a 2–2 draw.

Answers

1. French.
2. Argentina.
3. Stuart Roberts.
4. QPR.
5. 7–1.
6. Jason Jones.
7. Roger Freestone and Nick Cusack.
8. Brian Flynn.
9. Damien Lacey.
10. Walsall.

Anagrams

Fact: when the history of the Swans is finally written, a manager with the anagram 'Hailed Puma Curl' will have a significant chapter written for him. See beneath the answers below for his identity.

The following are all anagrams of managers of Swansea Town/City, in either a full-time or caretaker capacity.

1. Fry Thighs Friar

2. Nerd Orders? Bang!

3. Hot Nosh Jack?

4. A Usual Oops!

5. Lank Orca

6. Social Odd Inn

7. My Cask Maid

8. Platoon Pencil

9. Try Retro Hay!

10. Manly Job

Did you know?

The anagram 'Brawn For Rusk' is quite suitable for this manager. An honourable man, he had played his football in a tough period for the game and he carried his no-nonsense approach into management.

Played for both!

Fact: *having managed the Swans on two occasions, Terry Yorath joined the select band who have managed both Swansea and Cardiff when he took the Bluebirds' hot seat in 1994.*

The subject of every question of this quiz have represented both the Swans and Cardiff City.

Questions

1. Who was the 30-year-old Welsh international centre back who was signed from Cardiff City in August 1989 after previously having played for Spurs, Crystal Palace, Wimbledon, Bristol City and Newport County?

2. Which striker, signed by Swansea City from non-league in 1991, made 43 league appearances for Cardiff in 1998 before rejoining the Swans in 2001?

3. Who was the forward who left the Swans for Birmingham City in 1995 then, after spells at Southampton and Reading, joined Cardiff in 1999, where he made 135 league appearances?

4. Who scored 75 goals in 162 league appearances with Cardiff up to November 1970, then scored 25 league goals in 63 games for the Swans between 1978 and 1984?

5. Which Caerphilly-born striker scored 10 goals in 56 Swansea league appearances from 1994–97, then five goals in 31 Cardiff appearances between 1998 and 2000?

6. Which 21-times capped Swansea-born centre half played for Arsenal from 1946, Sunderland from 1953 and Cardiff from 1957 before finally joining Swansea and returning home in 1958, playing 44 league games with seven goals?

7. Which Cardiff striker joined Portsmouth in 1989 for £215,000 before moving on to the Swans in 1990 for £125,000? His career was ended by a back injury.

8. Which Swans defender, who played 228 league games for the club before moving to Gillingham in 1995, signed for Cardiff in 1997, playing 38 games?

9. Who was the player with strong family Swansea connections who joined Cardiff from school, making 211 league appearances before joining Blackburn in 1966, then joining the Swans from Aston Villa in 1970 before retiring in 1972?

10. A former Swans centre half between 1976 and 1978, this popular figure then managed Cardiff between 1991 and 1994 and again from 1995–96.

The 2000s

Fact: *most people see the final Hull City game of the 2002/03 season as critical in the club's survival, which it was. But if the Swans had lost the previous game away at Rochdale, they would still have been relegated. Crucially, it was won 2–1.*

Questions

1. Which Swans midfielder received a straight red card in the opening game of the 2002/03 season against Rushden & Diamonds at the Vetch?

2. Who was the 20-year-old striker signed on loan from Blackburn Rovers in November 2002, who played 17 league games in the season, scoring seven goals?

3. Which shirt number was Leon Britton handed for the rest of the season after he was signed on loan on 2 December 2002?

4. Which young midfielder, who had joined the club from Llanelli in 2000, made his final appearance for the club away at Shrewsbury in April 2003?

5. Which experienced midfielder was signed from Bury on 24 January 2003, made his Swans debut the next day at the Vetch and played a vital role in securing the Swans' safety by the end of the season?

6. Which player was signed by the Swans on loan from Manchester United in November 2002, signed again on loan in October 2003 before signing permanently in February 2004?

7. Kenny Jackett was appointed manager of the club in April 2004, but which club did he leave as assistant manager to take over the reins at the Vetch?

8. Who was the club's leading scorer in 2003/04 with 21 goals in all matches?

9. Which player wore the number 8 shirt throughout the 2003/04 season, making 31 league appearances, plus eight as sub and scoring eight goals?

10. Who was the 21-year-old former West Ham United trainee who joined the Swans from the Hammers in August 2003 and played 34 league games for the club in the 2003/04 season?

Did you know?

The season following the club's 'Great Escape' against Hull City, the Tigers returned to the Vetch – again late in the season – in 2004. This time Hull had their revenge, winning 3–2 and sealing their promotion.

Debuts

Fact: in the opening game of the 1938 season, away at Manchester City, the Swans picked five players for their club debuts – Bamford, Chedgzoy, Imrie, Rhodes and Bruce. Unfortunately, it wasn't a lucky five for the debutants as the Manchester club racked up five goals of their own, with no reply from the Swans. All five kept their places for the next game though, a 1–1 away draw at Bradford Park Avenue.

Questions

1. Which central defender and future Cardiff City manager made his debut for the Swans in a 4–1 League Cup home win over Newport County on 14 August 1976?

2. Who was the former England captain who was given the Swans captaincy on his debut against Huddersfield Town on 17 September 1983, a game that was lost 1–0? He played the next six games before leaving the club for good.

3. Which left-sided player made his debut as a 22-year-old against Bristol City in a 2–0 away defeat on 1 October 1988? He made 162 league appearances for the club before making a similar number for Cardiff City later in his career.

4. Can you name the striker, with over 50 caps for Jamaica, who made a scoring debut for the club, netting both goals in a 2–0 victory over Rotherham United at the Vetch on 12 October 1999?

5. Who was the goalkeeper, signed on loan from Stoke City, who made his league debut for the club on St David's Day 2003, keeping a clean sheet in the 0–0 game with Wrexham at the Vetch?

6. Which versatile defender, who would win over 50 full caps for Wales, made his Swans debut on 7 August 2004 in a 2–0 home defeat against Northampton Town?

7. On the opening day of the 2006/07 season against Cheltenham Town at the Liberty, Kevin Amankwaah, Tom Butler and which midfielder – who would make 177 league appearances for the club – all made their debuts for the club?

8. Which member of the current Premier League squad made his debut – initially on loan – away at Carlisle on 8 April 2008, in a 0–0 draw?

9. Who was the striker who made his debut for the club against Colchester United at the Liberty Stadium in the third round of the FA Cup on 8 January 2011?

10. Which on-loan international midfielder made his club debut when he came on as substitute for Andrea Orlandi in the third round of the FA Cup at Barnsley on 7 January 2012?

Did you know?

The 1949/50 season saw the debuts of two long-serving brothers and loyal servants to Swansea Town. The first was Cyril Beech, scoring the winner against Sheffield United at the Vetch on 1 September 1949 following his move from Merthyr Town. Then, four months later, his older brother Gilbert, who had also signed from Merthyr, made his bow against Southampton, not scoring, but also tasting victory on his debut.

Answers

1. Eddie May.
2. Emlyn Hughes.
3. Andy Legg.
4. Walter Boyd.
5. Neil Cutler.
6. Sam Ricketts.
7. Darren Pratley.
8. Ashley Williams.
9. Luke Moore.
10. Gylfi Sigurdsson.

Who am I?

Below are ten facts about a former Swansea City player. You get 10 points if you guess who it is from the first fact, and all the way down to one point if you don't guess correctly until the tenth fact. Answer given at the bottom – no peeking!

Facts

1. I was born in 1968.

2. I played for two Welsh clubs in the Football League.

3. I played for Wales at schoolboy, Under-21s, B and full international level.

4. I first played for Swansea City in 1989.

5. I scored three league goals for the club in my 14 seasons with Swansea.

6. In 2002 I released a book about my career called *Another Day At The Office*.

7. After an initial loan spell from a London club, I signed for the Swans for the 1991/92 season. I only missed seven league games in my first six seasons with the club.

8. I won my only senior Wales cap in the 2000 international against Brazil.

9. I was once joint manager of Swansea City for a short period with Nick Cusack.

10. I have made more appearances for the Swans – in all competitions – than any other player in the club's history. And I am a goalkeeper.

> **Did you know?**
> The holder of most league appearances for Swansea
> City, defender Wilf Milne, played in every position
> for the club, even goalkeeper.

Answers

Roger Freestone

The Premier League Season Two 2012/13

Fact: *the last Premier League home game the Swans won the during the season was on 2 March 2013 against Newcastle United in a 1–0 win, with the winner coming from Luke Moore.*

Questions

1. Which player scored his final goal for the club in the opening day victory at QPR?

2. How many games did the Swans win in the league during their second season?

3. Which team gave the Swans their first home defeat of the season in a 3–0 reverse on 22 September 2012?

4. Michu was the club's highest league scorer with 18, but which two players were next on the list with five each?

5. Which player made the most league appearances during the season with 37?

6. Against which three teams did the Swans 'do the double', beating them home and away?

7. Which team inflicted Swansea's heaviest defeat, 5–0, in an away game?

8. Which squad number did Chico Flores wear throughout the season?

9. The most bookings received by a player in the Premier League was seven, achieved by which two defenders?

10. The Swans made three loan signings for the season. Jonathan de Guzman was one, Itay Shechter another, but who was the third, who signed on 15 January 2013?

Did you know?

In terms of minutes played in the Premier League during the season, Mark Gower played the fewest, with just six minutes, after coming on as an 84th minute substitute for Michu in the season's opener against Queens Park Rangers.

The 2000s

Fact: *in the 2005/06 season, the Swans scored more than three goals in a match on five occasions: four against Rushden & Diamonds and Chesterfield, five against Walsall and Chesterfield, and seven against Bristol City.*

Questions

1. Which player joined the Swans from Torquay United in July 2005 and went on to score 15 goals in all football from 44 appearances in his debut season?

2. Owain Tudur Jones joined the Swans in the pre-season of 2005/06 for a £5,000 fee, but which Welsh League club did he join the club from?

3. In their third away game back in League One in the 2005/06 season, the Swans won 5–2 away at Walsall. Which former Walsall player opened the scoring for the Swans that day after 15 minutes?

4. Just two weeks after that high-scoring Walsall win, the Swans put seven past Bristol City at home. Which winger marked the game with a hat-trick?

5. Which striker scored his own Liberty Stadium hat-trick, on his debut against MK Dons on 10 January 2006?

6. Who beat the Swans in the 2006 League One play-off final at the Millennium Stadium?

7. Which two players scored for the Swans in that 2–2 drawn final?

8. And which two Swans players missed penalties in the doomed penalty shoot-out?

9. The Swans signed defender Kevin Amankwaah in July 2006 for a reported £250,000, from which club?

10. Striker Rory Fallon was sold by the club in January 2007 for a fee believed to be in excess of £300,000. Who was he sold to?

Did you know?
In the 2006 League Trophy final, a player who played the full 90 minutes was a loan signing defender who only ever played six games for the Swans and went back to his parent club two weeks later. His name? Keith Lowe.

Answers

1. Adebayo Akinfenwa.
2. Bangor City.
3. Roberto Martinez.
4. Kevin McLeod.
5. Leon Knight.
6. Barnsley.
7. Rory Fallon and Andy Robinson.
8. Adebayo Akinfenwa and Alan Tate.
9. Yeovil Town.
10. Plymouth Argyle.

The teams

Can you recognise the Swans' players below from the clubs that have made up their careers? The dates relate to their career span and an asterisk (*) denotes a loan spell.

1. 1950–1964: Cardiff City, Manchester United, Swansea Town, Newport County.

2. 1971–1986: Halifax Town, Liverpool, Leicester City, Swansea City, Newport County, Mansfield Town, Hartlepool United, Peterborough United, Hartlepool United, Swansea City.

3. 1989–2008: Millwall, Bradford City, Swansea City, Bristol City, Notts County*, Scunthorpe United, Lincoln City.

4. 2001 – present: Tortosa, Reus, Girona, Saint Andreu, Terrassa, Swansea City.

5. 1983–1996: Swansea City, Sunderland, Swansea City*, Swansea City, Blackpool.

6. 1995–2013: Torquay United, Southampton, Torquay United*, Stockport County*, Oxford United*, Sheffield Wednesday*, Barnsley*, Barnsley, Swansea City.

7. 1973–1993: Swansea City, Stoke City, QPR, Leicester City, Swansea City, Bradford City, Cardiff City.

8. 1999–2011: Red Star 93, Le Mans, Millwall, Swansea City, MK Dons.

9. 1984–2000: Stirling Albion, St Mirren, Swansea City.

10. 1991–2004: Southampton, Hull City*, Stockport County, Lincoln City*, Swansea City, Oxford United*, Oxford United.

Did you know?
Jason Bowen made over 100 appearances for three different Welsh clubs – Swansea, Cardiff and Newport. He also played for Birmingham City, Southampton and Reading.

Answers

1. Colin Webster.
2. Alan Waddle.
3. Steve Torpey.
4. Angel Rangel.
5. Colin Pascoe.
6. Garry Monk.
7. Robbie James.
8. Willy Gueret.
9. Keith Walker.
10. Matthew Bound.

A to Z – the letter A

All the answers in this quiz are surnames of former
Swans players which begin with the letter A.

Questions

1. Made his first team debut in February 1951 in
   Welsh Cup versus Pembroke Borough. Had two
   Swans spells, 1950–61 and 1969–71, making over
   350 appearances. Also played for Sheffield United,
   Stockport County and 11 times for Wales.

2. Signed for the Swans from Bristol Rovers in March
   1998 and scored 16 league goals in 90 appearances
   before leaving for Cheltenham. In 1999 scored
   club's fastest ever hat-trick, versus Cwmbran in
   Welsh Premier Cup – four minutes.

3. Full back signed from Cardiff in 1979. 100+ games
   for Swans, Toshack didn't fancy him in his Division
   One team, so was sold to Derby County in
   February 1982.

4. Signed from Ipswich as a 20-year-old midfielder by
   Jan Molby in 1996, stayed at club making 120 league
   appearances before moving to Kidderminster in
   2001. Was sent off three times in 1997/98 season,
   twice in succession!

5. Left-sided player signed from Cefn Hengoed
   school, who went on to play over 50 games for the
   club between 1984 and 1988 after making debut
   as a 16-year-old against Shrewsbury in Welsh Cup
   semi-final.

6. No-nonsense defender signed by Kenny Jackett in 2004, played both left back and centre back. Played over 100 league games for the Swans before joining Chesterfield in 2008. Played seven times for Trinidad and Tobago.

7. Former Arsenal trainee, left-sided midfielder signed from West Bromwich Albion in 1994. Played at Wembley for the Swans in both Autoglass final in 1994 and play-off final in 1997. Became first player to leave Swans on a 'Bosman' in 1998, joining Leyton Orient.

8. Popular north-east-England-born striker, scored in seven consecutive games in 1987/88 season, with a spectacular scissors kick against Cardiff in 1988 especially memorable. Surprisingly sold to Hartlepool in November 1988.

9. Signed for Swans aged 15 after leaving Plasmarl school. First capped for Wales aged 21, played 26 consecutive times in total of 68 caps. Legend.

10. Experienced ex-Southampton left back, signed in 1991, made debut versus Cardiff in FA Cup, then played them again in Autoglass Cup three days later. Often captain, made nine appearances for Nigeria. Left Swans in 1993 after 35 games.

> **Fact:** *Swansea City scored ten goals in their first three Premier League games of the season and none in the next three.*

Questions

1. The most goals the Swans conceded in a home Premier League game was four, in a game in which they scored three themselves. But who were their opponents?

2. One of the Swans' players was given a straight red card during the season, but who was the only player sent off in the league during the season for two bookable offences?

3. Which player suffered a broken ankle in the home game against Sunderland?

4. Which player left the club in the January transfer window after making ten starts and seven substitute appearances in the League?

5. How many goals did Michu score in all competitions?

6. From which club did the Swans sign Ki Sung-yueng?

7. Which player left the club during the season for a fee reported to be £6.2 million?

8. Which player's squad number throughout the season was number 11?

9. Ashley Williams made the most starts in the League with 37, but who was second with 34 starts?

10. Who did the Swans face in their final league game of the season, played at home on 19 May 2013?

Did you know?
Leroy Lita was loaned to two teams during the season, Birmingham City and Sheffield Wednesday.

Honours

Questions

1. In the League Cup final win of 2013, who scored the Swans' first goal?

2. Which player was captain for Swansea in the 2011 Championship play-off final?

3. Which division did Swansea Town win in 1924/25 and again in 1948/49?

4. Which midfielder was club captain during the 1999/2000 season, when the Swans finished the season as champions of the fourth tier of English football?

5. When Swansea won promotion to the Championship in 2008 as champions of League One, they had three players who represented a Caribbean nation. Can you name this country?

6. Can you name the three players concerned?

7. The furthest the Swans have ever got in the FA Cup is the semi-final on two occasions. Which team did they lose to the last time, in 1964?

8. Swansea City last won the Welsh Cup in 1991, for the tenth and final time, beating Wrexham 2–0. But who managed the Swans to that victory?

9. Due to winning the 2013 League Cup, Swansea qualified for the Europa League. Following the qualifying rounds, in which stadium did they play their first group match on 19 September 2013?

10. What nationality was Swansea's goalkeeper in the 2013 League Cup final?

Did you know?
Swansea City fielded four loan players in their League One championship-winning season of 2007/08. They were: Paul Anderson (Liverpool), Febian Brandy (Manchester United), Warren Feeney (Cardiff City) and a certain Ashley Williams (Stockport County).

Answers

1. Nathan Dyer.
2. Garry Monk.
3. League Division Three (South).
4. Nick Cusack.
5. Trinidad and Tobago.
6. Kevin Austin, Denis Lawrence and Jason Scotland.
7. Preston North End.
8. Frank Burrows.
9. The Mestalla (Valencia).
10. German (Gerhard Tremmel).

Loan Rangers

Below is a list of players who signed on loan for the Swans at some point during their careers. Can you recognise them from the details given?

Questions

1. A French striker signed on loan from Paris St Germain in February 2001, scored three league goals in 12 games; two of them in a 6–0 win over Brentford.

2. A striker loaned from Reading in August 2001, in eleven appearances in the league he scored one goal, got injured and missed two games, and then was sent off as a second-half substitute against Kidderminster Harriers.

3. A goalkeeper signed on loan from Stoke City in February 2003, played 13 league games for the Swans, including a crucial role in the fight to avoid relegation to the Conference.

4. Son of a Welsh international winger, signed on loan from Manchester United in October 2003, playing four league games. Scored the only goal in LDV Vans Trophy v Southend United.

5. Winger, originally came on loan from Bristol City in November 2004 before signing full-time in June 2005. In his loan spell, scored three goals in six league games.

6. Loaned by Portsmouth, although came via Coventry following a previous loan spell in January 2007. Signed as a central defender, had previously played at full back for the Swans prior to leaving in January 2004.

7. Striker, signed in March 2011 from Chelsea, scoring six goals in nine games before leaving the club on 31 May the same year.

8. Midfielder, signed on a season long loan from Espanyol for 2008/09 season. Made 44 league appearances, scoring 12 goals.

9. Canadian-born defender, loaned from Burnley in March 2010, making five league starts and scoring in the 3–0 home win over Scunthorpe.

10. Welsh international forward, loaned from MK Dons for a month in December 2010, scoring once in two full league games and four substitute appearances.

Trunds

> **Fact:** Lee 'Trunds' Trundle became the first ever official Club Ambassador when he was appointed to the role in June 2013.

Questions

1. Can you name any one of the five English non-league clubs that Trunds played for?

2. Which Welsh Premier League club did Trunds join in 2000?

3. Which Football League team did Trunds join after impressing for his Welsh Premier League club by scoring 15 times in 18 games?

4. Who was the manager who brought Trunds to Swansea in the summer of 2003?

5. Trunds scored on his Swans debut against Bury in August 2003, with Brad Maylett scoring a hat-trick in the same game. But in the very next league game away from home, Trunds scored his own debut hat-trick in a 4–3 win. Against whom?

6. Due to the flamboyant nature of his all-round play, Trunds became a regular on which Sky TV programme?

7. In the 2006 Football League Trophy final, Trunds scored a spectacular volley after just three minutes. Who was Trunds' strike partner, who scored the winner to beat Carlisle?

8. In his first spell with the Swans, Trunds made 146 league appearances, scoring better than a goal every other game. How many goals did he score?

9. Which team did Trunds join for £1 million in 2007?

10. In Trunds' final spell with the club, he made 20 appearances scoring five goals. But how many of those appearances were starts, as opposed to substitute appearances?

Did you know?
In 2005, Trunds signed an image rights contract with the Swans, becoming the first player outside of the Premier League to do so.

Answers

1. Burscough, Chorley, Stalybridge Celtic, Southport and Bamber Bridge.
2. Rhyl.
3. Wrexham.
4. Brian Flynn.
5. Cheltenham Town.
6. Soccer AM.
7. Adebayo Akinfenwa.
8. 78.
9. Bristol City.
10. Two.

SWANSEA CITY AFC

The Premier League Season Three 2013/14

Fact: in the 4–0 home win against Sunderland on 19 October, the Swans were credited with two own goals by the Premier League dubious goals panel – the first by Phil Bardsley in the 57ᵗʰ minute and the second by Steven Fletcher in the 80ᵗʰ minute.

Questions

1. Who scored the Swans' first league goal of the season?

2. Which two players scored the Swans goals in the first league win of the season, a 2–0 victory over West Bromwich Albion at the Hawthorns on 1 September?

3. Against which team did Michu score his first league goal of the season, on 16 September?

4. Who knocked the Swans out of the League Cup on 25 September?

5. Which player was penalised for an extremely controversial handball at the end of the match with Stoke City at the Liberty on 10 November, allowing Charlie Adam to convert a last minute penalty, earning his side a 3–3 draw?

6. What was significant about Hull City's goal at the Liberty in the 1–1 draw on 9 December?

7. In which away game during the season did the Swans enjoy an incredible 73 per cent possession and have 17 shots, winning eight corners, but only drawing the game 1–1?

8. Which shirt number was David N'Gog given when he joined the club in January 2014?

9. Which Premier League match was Michael Laudrup's final one in charge of the club?

10. Who scored the opening goal in the comprehensive 3–0 victory over Cardiff City in head coach Garry Monk's first game in charge?

Did you know?
In their qualifying group for the Europa League, Group A, the Swans conceded the fewest number of goals of all four teams, letting in just four. And of those four, two of them were conceded in stoppage time.

Can you name all these players? Answers on p. 153

1.

2.

3.

4.

5.

6.

7.

8.

9.

10.

Where are they now?

Can you name the former Swans from the clues about their Swans career and the jobs they currently do? All facts in this quiz are correct as at 15 September 2014.

Questions

1. Which defender, who won 89 international caps and played for the Swans in 79 league games between 2006 and 2009, is now a member of Roberto Martínez's backroom staff at Everton?

2. Initially on loan, this striker was a £200,000 signing in 2007, but the move to Swansea never really worked out, scoring just once in 20 league games after his permanent transfer. Now plays in the Indian Pro League for Salgaocar in Goa.

3. Which midfielder who, despite only spending a short, injury-plagued 17-game spell at the club between 2006 and 2008, was well-liked and respected, is now first team coach of Yeovil Town?

4. Which striker, originally signed in 2003, scored 16 league goals for the club and is now assistant manager at Leyton Orient, a post he also held for the Swans?

5. Signed during the crucial 2002/03 season, this defensive midfielder took part in the critical Hull City game, and played 40 league games in the darkest period of the club's recent history. He is now a primary school teacher in Lancashire.

6. Which keeper played 99 league games for the club after signing from West Ham United, and gave a heroic performance against Liverpool in the FA Cup in 1990? He's now a neighbourhood PC for Greater Manchester Police in Rochdale South.

7. A much-travelled South American striker, who scored 12 goals in 31 league appearances during the 2000/01 season before joining Millwall. He is now head coach and sporting director of New York Cosmos.

8. Striker signed from Bradford City in 1993, and scored 44 league goals in 162 games, before joining Bristol City. He is currently assistant manager at York City.

9. A nine-times capped Nigerian international, this defender had previously played for Sunderland before playing 28 league games for the Swans in the early 1990s. Since 2005, he has been a manager at Parkway Car Sales in Southampton.

10. Injury ended this popular and much-travelled striker's career at Swansea in 1993, but not before he had become a fans' favourite – not easy for an ex-Cardiff player – by scoring 23 league goals in 62 games. Recently head coach at the NIKE Football Academy in the FA's new St George's Park complex, he is now lead professional development coach at Nottingham Forest.

Answers

1. Dennis Lawrence.
2. Daryl Duffy.
3. Darren Way.
4. Kevin Nugent.
5. Lenny Johnrose.
6. Lee Bracey.
7. Giovanni Savarese.
8. Steve Torpey.
9. Reuben Agboola.
10. Jimmy Gilligan.

Swansea boys

Swansea have always had a long and proud tradition of producing local talent for the first team, but can you identify the local products who have had a significant impact on the club's history from their mini biographies below?

Questions

1. Versatile player who made his first team debut as an 18-year-old in August 2009 in 3–0 defeat by Middlesbrough. Has played for Swans in Premier League and also won first full Welsh cap in 2012. In 2013, signed a contract to keep him at club until 2016.

2. Born in 1923, his only full league season with the club saw him score nine goals in 16 games. However, in the previous 1945/46 season, an unofficial league because of World War Two, he scored 41 goals in 43 games. The winner of 38 Wales caps, he was one of Wales' greatest goalscorers. Passed away in Swansea in 2003.

3. One of the club's most talented attacking players, signed by John Toshack in 1980 for £130,000. Had begun his career away from Swansea as an apprentice at Burnley, and finished it there in 1986. But in 98 league games for the Swans, with many match-winning performances in the top division, he remains one of the club's best ever wide-men.

4. Cultured defender who could also operate in midfield, made his debut as a 16-year-old in the FA Cup in 1985. Over the next five seasons, he would make 175 league appearances and break onto the Wales squad. Played for another six league clubs before finishing his career in 2005, having made over 700 league appearances and winning 65 Welsh caps.

5. Began as an apprentice at Birmingham City in 1971 before returning to his home town in 1985 after spells at Bristol Rovers, Swindon Town, Newport County and Bristol

City. A consistent, hard-working midfielder who made over 130 appearances for the club until 1988, his father and uncle had also played for the Swans, in the 1930s.

6. Left Swansea for Manchester in 1955, joining the juniors of Manchester United, becoming one of their legendary Busby Babes. Returned to Swansea in 1961, playing 54 league games for the club and scoring eight goals before joining Newport County in 1964.

7. A local boy who generated over £8 million in transfer deals during his career which stretched from 1983 to 2001. An FA Cup, League Cup and Turkish Cup winner, he scored 190 league goals in 618 appearances, with 12 of those coming in his 49 games for the Swans.

8. A genuine club legend who made 341 Football League appearances scoring 36 goals, having already played for the club in the Southern League in 1919. Retired in 1931, remaining in Swansea an running a thriving local business. Died in 1983, aged 86.

9. The captain of the Swans in one of their only two FA Cup semi-finals, the Preston game in 1964. Played over 200 games for the club, before leaving for Worcester City in 1966. Sadly, this cultured defender died aged just 50 in 1991.

10. Left-sided midfielder who played enjoyed two spells with the Swans, from 1993–2002, when he was released by Nick Cusack, only to re-join from Woking in March 2003. In total, made 296 appearances for the club scoring 18 goals, and had an assist in a memorable goal in the Hull City game in May 2003.

Answers

1. Jazz Richards.
2. Trevor Ford.
3. Leighton James.
4. Andy Melville.
5. Gary Emmanuel.
6. Ken Morgans.
7. Dean Saunders.
8. Billy Hole.
9. Mike Johnson.
10. Jonathan Coates.

Moving Out

Fact: *the grass isn't always greener for players leaving the Swans. After joining the club in 2007, Dorus de Vries hardly missed a game, racking up 178 league appearances in just four seasons. But in the three seasons since he left the Liberty, he has added only another 17 league games to his career statistics.*

Questions

1. Andy Legg is one of the many players who have represented Cardiff City after leaving the Swans, but which club did he go to first when he left the Vetch in July 1993 for £275,000?

2. In March 1996, one the Swans most popular ever players, John Cornforth, was sold by the club for £350,000. But which club did he join?

3. Adrian Forbes will always have the honour of scoring the last ever league goal at the Vetch on 30 April 2005. But which manager released Forbes in 2006, a move that bitterly upset the player and saw him signing for Blackpool as a free agent?

4. Since leaving the Swans in 2007, which player, who had made 61 league appearances for the club, has played for Millwall, Northampton Town (twice), Gillingham (twice), and his current club, AFC Wimbledon?

5. Following a promising loan period, Daryl Duffy joined the Swans from Hull City in 2007 for £200,000. However, after scoring just one goal in 20 league games as a permanent player, the club moved Duffy on for £100,000 just a year later. Which club did he join?

6. Who was the loyal player, comfortable in midfield or defence, who had come through the youth ranks at

Swansea to play 284 league games for the club, then was released prior to the 2010/11 season, seeing his playing career out at Neath?

7. Which player, who had become a free agent in the summer of 2010, left the Liberty and signed a three-year contract with Sheffield United?

8. David Cotterill was a popular winger with the club before he was released in January 2012, joining Barnsley. But which club did he join after just 11 games for Barnsley, a club he made over 80 league appearances for before moving to Birmingham City for the 2014/15 season?

9. Striker Craig Beattie had his contract with the club cancelled by mutual consent in January 2012. But which was the Scottish Premier League team he subsequently joined as a free agent the following month?

10. Which club did Alejandro Pozuelo join for an undisclosed fee on 24 July 2014?

Did you know?
England international Ray Kennedy's Swans career came to an abrupt end in 1983 after several lacklustre performances saw him being released and joining Hartlepool in his native north-east. However, it was only years later that Kennedy – and the club – found out that the reason for Kennedy's sub-standard performances in a Swans shirt was, tragically, the onset of Parkinson's disease.

Answers

1. Notts County.
2. Birmingham City.
3. Kenny Jackett.
4. Adebayo Akinfenwa.
5. Bristol Rovers.
6. Kristian O'Leary.
7. Leon Britton.
8. Doncaster Rovers.
9. Heart of Midlothian.
10. Rayo Vallecano.

The Premier League Season Three 2013/14

Fact: *during a season in which many observers felt that Swansea suffered from the pressures of playing in the Europa League, the Swans played a total of 54 games, winning 17, drawing 13 and losing 24. Two players shared the record for appearing in most of those 54 games – Wilfried Bony and Jonathan de Guzman, with 48 each (including substitute appearances).*

Questions

1. Wilfried Bony scored the winner to knock Manchester United out of the FA Cup in the third round tie on 5 January 2014, but who had opened the scoring for the Swans in the 12th minute?

2. A week later, the Swans returned to Old Trafford in the Premier League, but what was the score?

3. Who scored the final goal to round off a comprehensive 3–0 victory over Cardiff City in Garry Monk's first game in charge on 8 February 2014?

4. The Swans were knocked out of the FA Cup in the fifth round – by which club?

5. Which defender made their first appearance of the season in that FA Cup defeat, but lasted only 31 minutes due to injury, and featured only twice more during the season?

6. Which three teams did the Swans do the double over in the Premier League, beating them home and away?

7. Which player scored the Swans' lone goal in their exit defeat in the Europa League, losing 3–1 away at Napoli?

8. Which position did the Swans end up in the 2013/14 Premier League table?

9. How many points did the Swans finish with in the 2013/14 season?

10. Who was the player who made his debut for the club in the final home game of the season, coming on as a substitute for Jonathan de Guzman in the 4–1 victory over Aston Villa?

Did you know?
The Swans received three red cards during the Premier League season of 2013/1. Michel Vorm received one, but Chico received two, seeing red against Crystal Palace and Chelsea.

Answers

1. Wayne Routledge.
2. Manchester United won 2–0.
3. Wilfried Bony.
4. Everton.
5. Kyle Bartley.
6. Sunderland, Fulham, Newcastle.
7. Jonathan de Guzman.
8. 12th.
9. 42.
10. Jay Fulton.

Picture Quiz Answers

Quiz One
1. Ivor Jones
2. Tony Cottey
3. Jordi Amat
4. Adebayo Akinfenwa
5. Joe Sykes
6. Kyle Bartley
7. Keith Barber
8. Paulo Sousa
9. Kenny Morgans
10. Bob Latchford & Alan Curtis.

Quiz Two
1. Dennis Lawrence
2. Angel Rangel
3. Mike Hughes
4. Richard Duffy
5. Jonjo Shelvey
6. Pat Lally
7. Roy Saunders
8. Fede Bessone
9. Steve Potter
10. Marc Goodfellow

Quiz Three
1. Wilf Milne
2. Ferrie Bodde
3. Alvaro Vazquez
4. Jimmy Rimmer
5. Reg Weston
6. Izzy Irieikpen & Garry Monk.
7. Shefki Kuqi
8. Ivor Allchurch
9. Dai Davies
10. James Thomas

Quiz Four
1. Nick Cusack
2. Darren Pratley
3. Jason Scotland
4. Alan Tate
5. Mark Gower
6. Roy Paul
7. Craig Beattie
8. Ashley Williams
9. Harry Griffiths
10. Mike Johnson

Bibliography

The following were an invaluable resource in confirming facts and figures offered as questions and facts in this book:

Swansea City official match day programmes – 1973 to date
Official Biography of The Swans – David Farmer
Swansea Town/City FC A–Y – Colin Jones
Swansea Moments – a hundred and one years of supporting the swans – Swansea University
Swansea Town & City Football Club – The Complete Record – Colin Jones
football-league.co.uk
premierleague.com
swanseacity.net
bbc.co.uk
scfcheritage.wordpress.com
espn.co.uk
espnfc.com
soccerbase.com
football-lineups.com
transferleague.co.uk
faw.org.uk
wfda.co.uk

Scan for the
Swans' official
website

Scan for the
Gomer Press
website